Penguins
OF THE WORLD

Penguins
OF THE WORLD

Text and Photographs by
Wayne Lynch

FIREFLY BOOKS

A Firefly Book

Published by Firefly Books Ltd. 2007

First printing

Publisher Cataloging-in-Publication Data (U.S.)
Lynch, Wayne.
 Penguins of the World / Wayne Lynch.
2nd ed.
Originally published, 1997.
[176] p. : col. photos. ; cm.
Includes bibliographical references and index.
Summary: An examination of the life cycle of the 17 species of penguins from around the world. Includes detailed information on anatomy, habitats, predators, mating and feeding habits, and egg and chick development.
ISBN-13: 978-1-55407-334-4   ISBN-13: 978-1-55407-274-3 (pbk.)
ISBN-10: 1-55407-334-0   ISBN-10: 1-55407-274-3 (pbk.)
1. Penguins. I. Title.
598.44 dc22   QL696.S473.L96   2007

Library and Archives Canada Cataloguing in Publication
Lynch, Wayne
 Penguins of the world / text and photographs by Wayne Lynch. -- 2nd ed.
Includes bibliographical references and index.
ISBN-13: 978-1-55407-334-4 (bound)   ISBN-13: 978-1-55407-274-3 (pbk.)
ISBN-10: 1-55407-334-0 (bound)   ISBN-10: 1-55407-274-3 (pbk.)
1. Penguins. 2. Penguins--Pictorial works. I. Title.
QL696.S473L96 2007   598.47   C2007-900818-6

Published in the United States by
Firefly Books (U.S.) Inc.
P.O. Box 1338, Ellicott Station
Buffalo, New York 14205

Published in Canada by
Firefly Books Ltd.
66 Leek Crescent
Richmond Hill, Ontario L4B 1H1

Cover and interior design by Lindsay Munro Smail

Printed in China

The publisher gratefully acknowledges the financial support for our publishing program by the Government of Canada through the Book Publishing Industry Development Program.

Title page: The Adélie penguin nests up to 77 degrees South, deeper inside the Antarctic Circle than any other penguin species.

Opposite: The colorful king penguin is arguably the most beautiful of the 17 species of penguins worldwide.

Front cover: emperor penguins

Front flap: king penguins returning to their colony

Back cover, clockwise from left: rockhopper penguin and chick; adult emperor penguin and chicks; king penguin chick

Acknowledgments

None of these three adult emperor penguins may be the parent of this young chick, which is begging for food.

To my wife Aubrey,
the woman of my dreams,
and
my friend Joe Van Os,
who made this book possible

This book would not have been possible without the generous assistance of many people. Rodney Russ of Southern Heritage Expeditions shared his census results on fiordland penguins and also hired me to work on a cruise to the subantarctic islands of New Zealand, where he got me ashore on storm-battered Macquarie Island to observe royal penguins. I learned firsthand the pinching power of a penguin's beak when New Zealander Dr. Chris Challies invited me to band little penguins with him. Penguin researchers Dr. P. Dee Boersma, Dr. Gordon Court, Dr. David Duffy and Peter Moore generously sent me valuable unpublished information on the penguins they had studied.

Others who contributed include the Marine Life Department at the West Edmonton Mall; Sea World of California in San Diego; Ian Gjertz, a biologist with the Norwegian Polar Institute; Cynthia Cheney, the publisher of Penguin Conservation; David Schoeling, the executive secretary of the International Association of Antarctica Tour Operators; and Victor O. Lagos San Martin, a biologist with the Chilean Forest Service who helped me to locate Humboldt penguins. David Gray of the Falkland Islands deserves special thanks for collecting, soaking and stirring a putrid mix of penguin remains so that I could examine the birds' skeletons. I would also like to acknowledge the help of my longtime friend Joe Van Os of Joseph Van Os Photo Safaris, who has hired me to lead many trips to the haunts of penguins, and Erin Sutton of Calgary's X-treme Elements, manufacturers of the custom outdoor clothing that has always kept me warm and dry.

Finding a laboratory that will carefully process film is the perpetual quest of every professional photographer. For many years, I have been fortunate to work with Walter Weber at Nova Photo in Calgary, who has always fussed over my film as if it were his own.

I owe thanks also to *Discover* magazine, which allowed me to reprint portions of a column that appeared in the April 1995 issue, and to Cambridge University Press, which granted permission to quote excerpts from Euan Young's wonderful book *Skua and Penguin: Predator and Prey*.

Two people cheerfully accepted the onerous task of reviewing the text for technical accuracy. Dr. Tony D. Williams, assistant professor of physiological ecology at Simon Fraser University, Canada, and the author of the 1995 authoritative book The Penguins, brought an encyclopedic knowledge of these birds to the task of editing. I was honored and grateful that he agreed to help. The other reviewer was naturalist/writer David Middleton, who once again displayed a perceptive eye in detecting faulty logic and weak arguments. Of course, I alone accept all responsibility for any errors that may have crept into the text.

Many thanks to Barbara Hopkinson, Tracy Read and Lindsay Smail. More than anything, this group of professionals has proven to me that publishing a book can be fun and does not need to be an exercise in frustration and disappointment.

Finally, this is the 27th book I have written, and for the 27th time, I have dedicated the book to my wife Aubrey Lang. Her unwavering support, encouragement and love are a constant source of strength. I owe her so much.

Gentoo penguins normally raise two chicks, but earlier in the day a skua had preyed upon the second chick.

The second largest penguin in the world, the king penguin can stretch its height to more than 3½ feet (1 m) when fully grown.

Contents

Rockhopper penguins preen each other in a courtship display. Mutual care is a way for birds to reinforce their bond and to remove external parasites.

Penguin Passion

I saw my first penguin in November 1989. The sun had gone down an hour before, and I was shivering on a concrete bleacher in a cold wind. Around me sat several hundred other people anxiously watching the surf curl across a sandy beach on Phillip Island, in southern Australia. I was there for the nightly "penguin parade," where, under the glare of spotlights, hundreds of little penguins waddle up the beach to their nesting burrows. Surrounded by garrulous tourists and assailed by loudspeakers blaring artificial excitement, it was possibly the worst way to see an animal for the first time.

Even so, the penguins were wonderful. As eminent paleontologist Dr. George Gaylord Simpson wrote: "Penguins are habit-forming, and I am an addict." Like Simpson, it now seems that I, too, am an addict. That night on Phillip Island, I never imagined that over the next 18 years, I would travel more than 313,000 miles (504,000 km), which would include seven trips to Antarctica as well as multiple journeys to the Galápagos Islands, Argentina, Chile, New Zealand and a dozen remote island clusters in the tempestuous Southern Ocean, in search of the 16 other species of penguins.

As I write these words, it is late September, and I am excitedly preparing for my second voyage on a Russian icebreaker that will venture deep into Antarctica's Weddell Sea. There, I will observe and photograph emperor penguins — among the most alluring of the Earth's creatures. But all of my adventures with those charming "feathered fish" we know as penguins have been memorable. I remember the searing heat of Chile's Atacama Desert one Christmas Day when my wife and I searched the crevices of a volcanic island for nesting Humboldt penguins. I also recall laughing into my snorkel as a Galápagos penguin darted past my mask in the

These inquisitive emperor penguins were returning to their breeding colony from the sea and they approached to within 3 feet (0.9 m) of the photographer.

left: This male rockhopper penguin screams a welcome to his mate, which is returning from a trip to the sea to feed their chick. The male is the sole guardian of the chicks during their first few weeks of life.

Perhaps 50,000 or more king penguins nest on Salisbury Plain on South Georgia. Before leaving for the sea to feed, great numbers of birds loaf along the beach in the early morning.

gin-clear waters of the equator, and I will never forget the black rock, white ice and golden light of the Antarctic Peninsula as a group of Adélie penguins porpoised across the bow of my Zodiac. With memories like these, how could I not become addicted to penguins?

It turns out that Simpson and I are not alone in our penguino-philia. Penguin watching on Phillip Island is now a multi-million-dollar business. Last year, more than 500,000 eager visitors packed the island's parking lot. Zoos discovered the popularity of penguins some 90 years ago, and today, the birds are among their top attractions. At least 274 zoos, from Singapore to Sweden, feature penguin exhibits. Topping the list are the United States and Japan. Each country has roughly 70 zoos with penguins in their collections. The most famous of these is the Penguin Encounter at Sea World of California in San Diego, which boasts the largest colony of antarctic penguins outside of the continent itself. The park has nearly 350 penguins of seven different species. The indoor exhibit, a 5,000-square-foot (465 m²) refrigerator, is kept at a constant 25°F (−4°C) and has five tons (4,500 kg) of snow blown into it every day to keep the birds chilled out.

At a time when the trend in films is toward dazzling special effects and lifelike animations, the penguin craze has overtaken even Hollywood. Who could have predicted that a small-budget French film by former ecologist Luc Jacquet chronicling a year in the life of the emperor penguin would receive worldwide critical acclaim and win an Academy Award for 2006's best documentary feature film? It's easy for me, an avowed critter junkie, to understand why *March of the Penguins*, a simple film about a flightless polar seabird, is so appealing. But why did the film tug at the heartstrings of so many people who had never thought about penguins before, some of whom did not even know where Antarctica was located? No doubt, the continent's crystalline beauty, the stunning cinematography and the soothing, trustworthy voice of narrator Morgan Freeman contributed to the film's overwhelming appeal and box-office success. But perhaps it was something deeper than that. Could it be that a film about penguins and the natural world was a timely reminder of the relatedness of all life on Earth? No one has the answer to this question, although it is certain that movie studios would love to crack the code and inundate us with imitations. No matter, I am pleased that penguins, for a time at least, have become a symbol of all that is special and valuable in nature.

Advertisers have eagerly capitalized on the appeal of penguins for decades. Besides promoting ice-cream treats, refrigerators and party ice, penguins are frequently used to sell tuxedos and other formal wear, and it's easy to understand why. As the famous ornithologist Robert Cushman Murphy wrote in 1936: "With singular unanimity, explorers have likened the Adélie penguin to a smart and fussy little man in evening clothes, with the tail of his black coat dragging on the ground...who walks with the roll and swagger of an old salt just ashore from a long voyage."

A fun-loving biologist friend of mine, Dr. Peter Carey, collects photographs of various commercial products from around the world that use the image of a penguin in their advertisements. Two unusual ones are a Japanese jam and a popular brand of Brazilian beer. Paperback books published by Penguin Books, of course, are familiar to many people. The story goes that when the publisher was searching for a logo with which to launch his new paperback series, his secretary suggested a penguin. The bird seemed to be a

The humanlike postures adopted by penguins such as this magellanic from southern Argentina are one reason people find this family of seabirds so endearing.

perfect choice, since it embodied the spirit of the series — "dignified flippancy."

Humankind's fascination with penguins goes back a long time. For many centuries, the Aborigines of Australia, the Yahgans of Tierra del Fuego, the Maoris of New Zealand and the Bantus of southern Africa were interested in penguins and were acquainted with them in a way that can occur only when they are lying on your dinner plate. European and American explorers had a similar interest in the birds. Beginning in the 1500s, virtually every voyage of exploration to the Southern Ocean included salted barrelfuls of penguins for the ships' larders. Even today, peasant fishermen in Peru and Chile kill Humboldt penguins to feed their families.

But most of us lead lives quite removed from the natural world of penguins, and the present-day popularity of the birds certainly cannot be explained by their edibility. No doubt, there are many things that endear penguins to us, not the least of which are their upright stance, unwary curious nature, comical waddling gait, large heads—many with golden crests or bright patches of color—and fluffy potbellied chicks that resemble overstuffed laundry bags. In his book *Penguins—Past and Present, Here and There*, George Gaylord Simpson offers even more reasons we may find penguins so appealing: "It is easy to think of many penguin activities in human terms. They fight with their neighbors; steal from each other; quarrel with their wives but also give them gifts of rare stones; divide chores between mates, sometimes quite unevenly; often take good care of the kids but sometimes neglect or even kill them; are frequently true, in their fashion, to mates but sometimes have affairs and often are, in effect, divorced and remarried; play games; shout; make messes—the list could be prolonged."

Indeed, since Simpson wrote these insightful words more than three decades ago, the list is much longer. Today, scientists are scrutinizing every penguin species in many of the most remote corners of the planet. Through their eyes, we have learned that the lives of penguins are far more interesting and complex than we ever imagined. Though Simpson playfully compared the lives of penguins with those of humans, the life of a penguin goes well beyond the realm of our common shared experience. It is a life rich in adaptations and behaviors quite unique from our own. In the

past 20 years, the rapid pace of satellite technology has added even more to our understanding of these remarkable seabirds. Today, it is possible to track penguins across the vast, featureless expanses of the open oceans, chart the remarkable depths and frequencies of their feeding dives, calculate the size and success of their catches and even use implanted transponders to monitor their visits to their chicks.

For the past 28 years, I have devoted my life to the study and photography of wildlife behavior, and no group of creatures has interested me more than penguins. In this book, I will share with you the discoveries I have made, both in the field and in the count-less pages of scientific journals, about how penguins survive from day to day, how they have often made me laugh and how I have been deeply saddened by the tragedies that befall them. Most of all, *Penguins of the World* is a book about life, and in it, penguins are the heroes and villains, the winners and losers.

In many penguin colonies, as in this gentoo colony in the Falk-land Islands, the ground quickly becomes trampled and denuded of vegetation. This may be one reason gentoos shift the location of their homes every few years.

CHAPTER ONE

Blueprint of a Penguin

Outliving the Dinosaurs

Seventy percent of the Earth's surface is covered by oceans, yet of the nearly 9,800 species of birds in the world, only 300 species—roughly 3 percent—are seabirds. Typically, these include the birds that spend most of their time on the ocean, where they obtain their food.

Seabirds vary greatly both in size and in lifestyle. They range from the tiny Wilson's storm-petrel (*Oceanites oceanicus*), a 1¼-ounce (35 g) "sea swallow" that I have watched flutter in near-gale-force winds and deftly pick plankton from the ocean's foaming surface, to the exquisite wandering albatross (*Diomedea exulans*), which soars thousands of miles on colossal wings that can span 11½ feet (3.5 m), the largest wingspan of any bird. The magnificent frigatebird (*Fregata magnificens*) is another kind of seabird, a black-feathered man-of-war that rules the warm waters of the Tropics and lives mainly by piracy. Among the seabird tribe, there is also the stiletto-beaked northern gannet (*Sula bassana*), which plummets like a feathered arrow from heights of 90 feet (27 m), striking the water at speeds up to 60 miles per hour (95 km/h). And, of course, there are the swift-swimming penguins, the largest of which is the 65-pound (30 kg) emperor. The emperor penguin can remain submerged longer than any other bird and plunges to depths greater than 550 yards (500 m), reaching down to a world as black as space, where the crushing pressure is 30 times greater than at the water's surface.

Penguins are flightless seabirds, and while it seems unusual for any bird to lack the power of flight, there are, in fact, many examples

It was early December in the Falkland Islands and these king penguins had just begun to court at the beginning of another breeding season.

of flightless birds. A few of them include the kakapo (*Strigops hab-roptilus*), a flightless parrot from New Zealand; the flightless cormorant (*Phalacrocorax harrisi*) of the Galápagos Islands; the Titicaca flightless grebe (*Rollandia microptera*) in Bolivia; and, of course, the familiar ostrich (*Struthio camelus*) of Africa. Even so, flightlessness is uncommon in birds, and the 17 species of penguins are the largest family of birds in which all members are flightless.

As recently as the turn of the century, the flightless penguins were believed to be the living link between birds and fish. In 1902, on the strength of this theory, three heroic men dragged two heavy wooden sleds across the ice during the black frozen depths of an antarctic winter on a harrowing 19-mile (30 km) trek to visit an emperor penguin colony at Cape Crozier, along the Ross Sea. Explaining their mission—to collect a sample of eggs—Dr. Edward Wilson, the expedition's chief scientist, wrote: "We are inclined to search among the emperor as being among the most primitive of penguins if not the most primitive of birds."

The hardships suffered by these men were later chronicled by expedition member Apsley Cherry-Garrard in his riveting book *The Worst Journey in the World*: "The penguins' calls reached us, and we stood there, three crystallized ragamuffins above the emperors' home....After indescribable effort and hardship, we were witnessing a marvel of the natural world, and we were the first and only men who had ever done so; we had within our grasp material which might prove the utmost importance to science...and we had but a moment to give."

The party quickly collected five eggs, killed three penguins to fuel their blubber stove, then headed back. By that time, the rigors of the journey were beginning to take their toll. Cherry-Garrard confided in his diary: "We on this journey were already beginning to think of death as a friend. As we groped our way back that night, sleepless, icy and dog-tired in the dark, the wind and the drift, a crevasse seemed almost a friendly gift." Then, when it seemed that the situation could not have gotten worse for the intrepid trio, it did. A blizzard struck. "It was blowing as if the world was having a fit of hysterics and the earth was torn in pieces," wrote Cherry-Garrard. "The horrors of that return journey are blurred to my memory, and I know they were blurred to my body at the time....It is extraordinary how often angels and fools do the same thing in this life, and I have never been able to settle which we were on this journey."

Sadly, the precious eggs collected by Wilson and his comrades failed to prove that the emperor was the primitive ancestor of all

Close relatives, the emperor penguin, pictured here, and the king are the two largest species of penguins. The less brightly colored emperor is the larger of the two.

One of the great birds of flight, the black-browed albatross seems far removed from the flightless penguin. Yet scientists now believe that penguins descended from the albatross group of seabirds.

penguins. Today, we know that penguins are an ancient order of birds dating back to the time of the dinosaurs. By 55 million years ago, penguins were already flightless and were completely adapted to a life in the ocean. Scientists believe that these flightless seabirds arose even earlier than this from an ancestor which could fly and that the transition took place somewhere in the southern hemisphere roughly 65 million years ago, about the same time the dinosaurs disappeared. At that time, the continents of Australia, Antarctica and South America were still linked together and strung across the Earth's southern pole. The climate was different then as well. Cool temperate conditions extended to the pole, Antarctica was home to a great array of land animals and plants, and the surrounding seas were much warmer than they are today.

The closest relatives of the penguins are the seabirds known as tubenoses, which today include the albatrosses, shearwaters, fulmars, petrels, storm petrels and diving petrels. Weighing just over five ounces (150 g), the diving petrels are among the smallest of the tubenoses. These birds use their wings both to fly in the air and to swim underwater. Researchers believe that the earliest ancestors of the penguin family were seabirds similar to diving petrels, although they may have been substantially larger and have weighed slightly more than two pounds (1 kg). That seems to be the critical weight beyond which a bird cannot use its wings as both aerial propellers and underwater paddles. At body weights greater than this, the increased surface area of the wings makes them cumbersome and ineffective underwater. One of two things can happen: the bird can retain its wings for flying alone and use its feet to propel itself underwater — a strategy adopted by cormorants, sea ducks and loons — or it can abandon aerial flight altogether in favor of enhanced underwater flying. Penguins adopted the latter. Once the earliest penguins were no longer constrained by the need to fly, the size of their bodies could get much larger. Many of them did just that.

When the dinosaurs disappeared, many marine reptiles also became extinct. The time was right for penguins, and they diversified rapidly to exploit the ocean vacancies left by the extinction of

these reptiles. In fact, from 40 to 25 million years ago, penguins were the dominant warm-blooded predators of fish, krill and squid. The penguin family was very different then. To begin with, there were at least 40 species compared with the 17 living today, and half of these were larger than emperor penguins. One of the largest was *Anthropornis nordenskjoeldi*, which stood up to 5 feet 7 inches (170 cm) tall and possibly tipped the scales at nearly 300 pounds (135 kg). Paleontologist George Gaylord Simpson quipped that "their height would not suffice for basketball, but their weight was about right for football."

The good life for the penguin clan did not last very long. The birds eventually found themselves with some very serious competition for the edible bounties of the sea. The first were small toothed whales, and they were followed by seals and sea lions. Both of these warm-blooded groups of predators could maneuver easily in the water and swim fast, and they ultimately ousted the larger penguins by outcompeting them. In the end, only the smaller penguins survived, and it is these that are with us today.

The common dolphin is one of the small toothed whales. the evolution of these aquatic predators 15 to 20 million years ago led to the disappearance of the largest penguins. Today, only the smaller species survive.

The wing bones in all penguins, including these magellanics coming ashore in Argentina, are fused together to form stiff, durable paddles that the bird uses to swim underwater.

The Basic Penguin

When the earliest ancestors of the penguin made the final transition from combined aerial and aquatic flight to flying only underwater, natural selection had a free hand to optimize the shape of their bodies, modify the structure of their wings, legs and feet and alter the design and distribution of their feathers so that the birds were as energy-efficient as possible. One December, I learned firsthand some of the ways that penguins have adapted to life in the sea.

In 1994, David Gray, the affable owner of Sea Lion Lodge in the Falkland Islands, presented me with a Christmas present: a bucket filled with water and the putrefying remains of an adult gentoo penguin and a magellanic penguin that he had scavenged from the beach. The penguin carcasses had been soaking for months, and most of the flesh had fallen away from the bones. As a result, I was able to examine the birds' skeletons in detail, something I had wanted to do for a long time, although it meant repeatedly stifling my gag reflex.

A penguin's skeleton is relatively easy to recognize, especially the bones of the wings, which are very distinctive. The wing bones are shorter than usual for birds, a number of them are fused together, and all of them are heavy and solid, lacking the typical air spaces found in those of flying seabirds. The dense bones make a penguin less buoyant, so it can dive more easily. This density also adds rigidity to the flipper, rendering it a more efficient paddle.

Using a stick to stir through the soupy mixture of my decaying bird carcasses, I lifted out a chest cage to examine it. A penguin's flippers are powered by two main groups of muscles. The largest of the two are the pectoral muscles, which attach to a deep keel on the front of the bird's chest. These provide power for the downstroke. A penguin also has strong muscles to elevate the flipper during the upstroke. The upstroke in flying seabirds is largely passive and creates very little forward propulsion. Penguins, on the other hand, generate power during both phases of flipper movement.

The force with which a penguin can wield its flippers is substantial, especially in the larger species. This fact is entertainingly demonstrated in the following account by Robert Cushman Murphy: "Five men from the Dundee whaler Balaena tried to overcome an emperor penguin without harming it and to hold it down on the ice. They were quite unequal to the task and were bowled over like ninepins. Eventually, they succeeded in strapping two leather belts around the bird's body, and standing back, they took a breath. So did the penguin—and burst the belts. The capable creature was finally secured with a rope, but when hoisted on board, it knocked out the ship's dog with a blow of its flipper."

An unusual bony spur is located roughly halfway around the curve of most of the penguin's ribs. About an inch (2.5 cm) long, the spur projects backward and rests on top of the neighboring rib. These ingenious struts probably add strength to the chest wall and distribute pressure, making the bird less vulnerable to compression injuries.

I learned a lot about penguins by also examining the bones of their legs. A penguin's legs are located as far back on its body as possible. In this position, they trail behind the bird when it swims, thus creating the least amount of drag while being optimally placed for steering. Because a penguin walks upright, its upper leg bones—the femurs—are quite short and are aligned horizontally

The shape of a penguin's beak determines the kind of prey it hunts. The king penguin uses its pincer like bill to catch squid and fish.

so that when the bird is standing, its knees are directly beneath its center of gravity. If the femurs were positioned more vertically, as they are in most other birds, the penguin would be perpetually off balance and forever falling forward, stabbing its beak into the ground.

It has often been observed that the penguin is among nature's best-dressed birds. Its tight coat of feathers looks like short fur, giving the penguin a sleek, well-groomed appearance. On most birds, the feathers are distributed over the surface of the body along tracts with featherless gaps in between. If you examine the dimple pattern on the skin of a plucked turkey, for instance, you will see what I mean. In penguins, however, the feathers are continuous, covering every square inch of the body surface. The density of feathers on a penguin's body is also greater than on any other bird — up to 80 feathers per square inch, which is three to four times that on any flying seabird of similar size. In addition, the individual feathers are small and lance-shaped, with a wispy collar of down at their base, and they overlap tightly like roofing tiles. All these feather features combine to produce a windproof outer shell that insulates the bird on land and to prevent cold water from seeping through to the penguin's skin and draining vital heat from its body when it is at sea.

On one of many trips to the Falkland Islands, I visited a colony of king penguins. Some of them were molting, and the ground was dusted like snow with shed feathers. The central shaft of the small feathers was stiff and springy and slightly bowed. Researchers believe that the feathers function like miniature springs, resisting compression so that when the bird dives underwater, an insulating layer of air is trapped under its feathers and is not squeezed out so readily by the water pressure. Even so, I have watched penguins swimming underwater, and they leave a visible trail of silver bubbles behind whenever they dive.

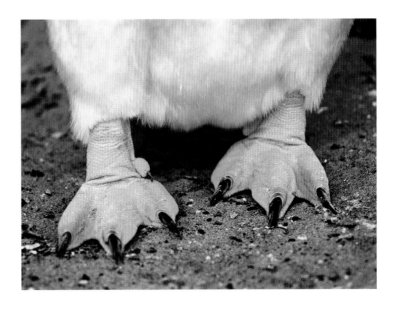

Like all penguins, the gentoo uses its webbed feet in combination with its tail and beak to steer underwater.

Another way the feather design may help the birds is by providing a protective padding, thereby shielding the penguins from injury during fights in which they exchange vigorous flipper blows. Likewise, they are cushioned when the seas are rough and they are tossed and battered against rocks on their trips ashore.

Penguins are very curious birds. If you stretch out quietly on the ground next to a gentoo colony when the chicks are nearly full-grown, the inquisitive youngsters will waddle over to investigate. That's how I got my first close look at a penguin's feet. Penguins have three large toes with webs between them and a small fourth toe at the rear of the foot, above the heel. In addition to the large size of their feet, it was their blunt, heavy claws that surprised me most, although they shouldn't have. Penguins use their claws to grip the surface of slippery algae-covered rocks when they come ashore, to propel themselves along when they are sliding on their bellies over the ice, to dig nesting burrows in hard soil and compacted guano and to provide traction when they are climbing slopes to their nesting colonies. The claws are so formidable that at rockhopper colonies on Steeple Jason Island in the Falklands, the clawed toes of countless generations of penguins have etched deep grooves into the rocks.

The torpedolike body of a gentoo penguin is common to all penguins and is the optimal shape for underwater travel.

Penguins on the Move

Penguins paddle, porpoise and flipper through the water, rocket and surf to reach the shore, then waddle, run, hop, leap and toboggan over the land. The penguin seems to have a greater range of ways to move than any other bird. Its versatility in the water and on land is perhaps a way to compensate for its flightlessness.

Penguins are seabirds, and as such, they are most at home on the water. Some species may spend three-quarters of their lives on the ocean. Fiordland crested penguins of New Zealand, for example, may bob around at sea so long that barnacles attach to their tails, and oceangoing African penguins sometimes have green algae growing on their backs from spending so many days in the water.

Swimming is, understandably, what a penguin does best. At the surface, it paddles with its webbed feet just as a duck does, but swimming like this is relatively slow and requires more energy—up to 4½ times more—than swimming underwater at the same speed. So when it's time to travel, a penguin goes under. As it darts through the water, 3 to 6½ feet (1-2 m) below the surface, its head is hunched between its shoulders and its body approaches a near-perfect torpedo shape that is propelled forward by its stiff paddlelike flippers. Considering the size and weight of a penguin, its flippers are relatively narrow and short. A Humboldt penguin and a golden eagle (*Aquila chrysaetos*), for example, weigh roughly the same, yet the surface area of the eagle's wing is 38 times greater than that of the penguin's flipper. The reason for this is that the eagle in flight must generate lift as well as forward movement, whereas the penguin, which is almost neutrally buoyant in the water, uses its flippers primarily for forward propulsion.

The earliest estimates of penguin swimming speeds were made by timing birds as they swam alongside a moving ship. These proved to be quite inaccurate. Using more sophisticated methods, sometimes in specially devised holding tanks, biologists have discovered that penguins *appear* to swim much faster than they actually do. The fastest swimmers are the large penguins—the kings and emperors. Emperors may streak along at 9 miles per hour (14 km/h), although they usually cruise at around 7 miles per hour (11 km/h). Mid-sized penguins, such as Adélies and chinstraps, commonly motor at 5 miles per hour (8 km/h), and little penguins travel at a leisurely 1 mile per hour (1.5 km/h), although they are

able to accelerate to 5½ miles per hour (8.5 km/h). To help put these speeds in perspective, consider the following: the fastest Olympic swimmers kick and splash along at just over 5 miles per hour (8 km/h), sea lions and fur seals sprint at 14 miles per hour (22 km/h), and tuna and sailfish, the fastest swimmers known, can accelerate to an exhausting 47 miles per hour (75 km/h).

If pressed, most penguins can travel faster by combining underwater sprints with low-level aerial leaps, a technique known as porpoising because of its resemblance to the familiar swimming style of porpoises and dolphins. A porpoising penguin arcs out of the water for a yard or so, takes an audible gasp, then plunges underwater again, often making a sudden change in direction. Usually, a penguin porpoises when it is near shore, moving to and from its nesting colony. This may be a strategy to outwit underwater predators, such as fast-swimming leopard seals, sea lions and killer whales, which regularly patrol the shoreline near penguin rookeries.

When a penguin leaps clear of the water, it is momentarily lost from view to an underwater predator. When it plunges in again and unexpectedly changes its direction of travel, it is difficult to

When a gentoo penguin rockets ashore out of the surf, it tries to stand on its feet as soon as it can, but the bird's momentum often results in a belly flop.

The rockhoppers in this small colony in the Falkland Islands were nesting above a steep cliff. to arrive at the cliff top, the birds had to scale a sheer rock face at a nearly 45-degree angle.

follow. I once watched a dramatic chase between a young South American sea lion bull (*Otaria byronia*) and a gentoo penguin. Both were porpoising, seemingly as rapidly as possible, but they would often surface separately. This was the key to the penguin's eventual escape. While the sea lion was airborne, the penguin could quickly change direction so that when the predator reentered the water again, it took an instant or two for it to relocate the bird and continue the pursuit. I suspect it was this repeated reorientation that allowed the penguin to gain a slight lead over the sea lion, which finally abandoned the chase.

I love to watch penguins come ashore. On the Falkland Islands, I've spent many relaxing hours and wasted innumerable rolls of film attempting to capture on celluloid the delightful sight of a penguin silhouetted inside the green translucency of a curling wave or momentarily riding its foaming crest. Even more challenging is trying to estimate where a bird will rocket out of the surf and flop onto its belly on the beach. The instant it lands, it scrambles to its feet and runs, seemingly to get away from the water's edge as quickly as possible. Then it often stops for a moment and looks back toward the water, as though asking itself what all the rush was about.

Rockhoppers and macaronis, two of the crested penguins, often land on steep, rocky, wave-battered shorelines. Typically, a wave spills the birds over the rocks, after which they immediately spring upright and begin frantically hopping upward. I wrote about some returning rockhoppers in my field notes: "The sea was a boiling froth that hammered the rocks and sent spray 90 feet [27 m] into the air, splattering the lens of my camera. Penguins landed in volleys, tossed around in the white foam at the base of the cliff as if they were churning in a kitchen blender. Frequently, after they hopped ashore, they stopped at the first flat rock to preen and straighten their ruffled plumage, only to have a large wave crash over the rocks and wash them back into the sea again."

Adélie penguins that nest on the ice-fringed coastline of Antarctica have their own set of landing problems. During the early half of the breeding season, a continuous skirt of ice is often anchored to the shore. As the tide falls, the ice becomes a formidable barrier. Sometimes, party after party of returning penguins launch themselves out of the sea only to crash against the ice cliff and fall back into the water. Some may succeed by leaping an impressive 6½ feet (2 m) or more into the air, three to four times their own height. When the returning tide raises the water level again, the barrier eventually disappears.

Once ashore, penguins lose the grace and agility they display in the water and adopt an energetic hop or the trademark swinging gait of Charlie Chaplin. These birds are not really designed for walking great distances. In fact, when king penguins first come ashore to molt, their bodies may be so padded with fat that it is difficult for them to walk at all. They may loaf around the shoreline for a few days before they finally labor inland to their molting grounds. Even when a penguin is not plumped up to molt, it uses considerable energy walking around. When a researcher compared the cost in energy of walking for an Adélie penguin and a domestic turkey of similar size, he concluded that the turkey strut took 42 percent less energy than the Adélie amble.

Penguins are likewise not great runners, and when extra speed is required, they have a simple way of boosting their getaway power. One of the first times I strolled on a sandy beach in Argentina, I encountered a small group of magellanic penguins. As I walked

A rockhopper can waddle, as most penguins do, but more often, it hops along in short bounds.

These tobogganing Adélie penguins had traveled over 10 miles (16 km) from the ice edge to reach their breeding colony on the Antarctic Peninsula.

closer to them, they began to run toward the water. When I didn't stop my approach, the birds fell forward on their bellies, their feet treading rapidly and their flippers flailing—the penguin version of four-wheel drive.

While ambulation is not their strength, penguins are capable walkers. Adélie and emperor penguins commonly travel close to 20 miles (30 km) across the sea ice to reach their breeding beaches. They could, of course, waddle the whole way, but instead, they lie down and cover much of the distance by "tobogganing" on their bellies, using their feet to shove them along while they keep their balance with outstretched flippers. Adélies can glide along like this at a couple of miles per hour, burning far less energy than if they were to walk upright.

Although all penguins regularly walk when they are on land, some of them also hop, especially one of the crested species, the appropriately named rockhopper. Of the rockhopper, Robert Cushman Murphy wrote: "Picture a penguin with a yellow pompon over each eye and a gait that caused the early visitors to the

Falklands to dub it the 'Jumping Jack.' Instead of walking, it progresses in a series of bounds executed with an elasticity of motion such as exhibited by a kangaroo."

But hopping gets the job done. Rockhoppers on Steeple Jason Island, in the Falkland Islands, scale slopes close to 500 feet (150 m) high, one six-inch (15 cm) hop at a time, taking an hour or more to reach their nesting colonies on top. If the slope becomes too steep, the resourceful birds use their hooked bills to grip the rocks and haul themselves up. In the end, it seems that neither imposing slope nor frightening surf nor any expanse of sea ice can deter a penguin on its way home.

To reach the steep, rocky shoreline of their nesting island, Snares penguins must often struggle through a thick tangle of bull kelp.

All in the Family

The name penguin was probably first used by sailors in the late 1500s in reference to the great auk, a large, flightless black-and-white seabird that lived in the cold waters of the North Atlantic and nested in colonies on remote islands. The derivation of the word is somewhat clouded, but possibly, it arose from the Latin word *pinguis,* which means fat. The scientific name for the great auk is *Pinguinus impennis*—the fat one without wings. Great auks stood about 2½ feet (75 cm) tall and were well padded with fat.

For centuries, European ships sailing to the New World stopped at the colonies of great auks to collect fresh eggs and kill the birds

Penguin tracks etch sand dunes in the Falkland Islands.

for storage in salted barrels. The last of these flightless seabirds was clubbed to death in Iceland in 1844. The confusion in names resulted because many of the same sailors later made voyages around the southern capes of Africa and South America, where they saw other flightless black-and-white birds, namely penguins. Upon seeing penguins for the first time, they naturally noted their resemblance to the great auk and called them by the same name.

Today, most authorities recognize 17 different species of penguins (see table on page 34). Basically, all of them are black or gray on the back and have a white chest and belly. This simple body coloration is the basis for the popular joke among naturalists on antarctic cruise ships, who quip that there are really only two kinds of penguins: the white ones approaching you and the black ones running away from you.

Naturalist Dr. Edward Wilson, who froze to death with Robert Falcon Scott while returning from their expedition to the South Pole in 1912, was the first to note that most penguins could be identified simply by the characteristic appearance of their heads and necks. These parts of the penguin are visible when it is floating quietly on the surface of the water. Biologists now believe that penguins use the same visual cues to recognize each other, which would account for the distinctive head and neck patterns, the differences in bill color and the presence of bright, conspicuous crests in many of the species.

Not everyone agrees that there are 17 kinds of penguins. As in all branches of biology, there are "lumpers" and "splitters"—those who tend to ignore differences and those who tend to emphasize them. Most of the controversy, however, revolves around the six species of crested penguins. Some critics believe that the erect-crested and Snares penguins are just races, or subspecies, of the fiordland penguin. They contend that there are only 15 species. Macaroni and royal penguins are also under scrutiny, and some researchers would lump them together as a single species. The most recent debate involves the rockhopper penguin, of which there are three subspecies. The northern race of rockhopper found on Île Saint-Paul and Tristan da Cunha, Gough and Amsterdam islands is different enough in body size, the length of its crest plumes and the color of its gape that some experts consider it to be a separate species, called Moseley's penguin. That distinction would raise the total count to 18. Until the smoke clears, I have settled on 17 species and adopted the classification found in *The Penguins,* Dr. Tony Williams' authoritative 1995 review of the family.

Like most people, you may take one look at the jumble of numbers in the table on the next page and decide that it would be more exciting to study a telephone directory. That may be a wise decision, but bear with me for a moment. I'd like to refer to some of the information in this table to make a few observations and to provide an overview of the penguin family. The 17 species in the penguin family belong to six groups, or genera. There are six kinds of crested penguins, all of which have conspicuous yellow or orange plumes above their eyes; four species of banded penguins, each of which has a single or double black-and-white band across its chest; three types of brush-tailed penguins, sporting stiff quilled tails much longer than those in the other species; two kinds of large penguins (the handsome emperor and king penguins); and the yellow-eyed and little penguins, each of which belongs to its own separate group.

The average body lengths listed for the different species represent measurements made from the tip of the bird's beak to the tip of its tail when it was stretched out flat on the ground. Of course, the height of a penguin when it is standing is a more interesting fact to know, since that is how we see them. Such measurements are unfortunately not available for most species. In general, however, the height of a penguin is roughly 85 percent of its body length. I have always wanted some easy way to compare the size of the different penguins, so I developed my own classification based on their

New Zealand's handsome yellow-eyed penguin is one of the most endangered of the 17 species of penguins worldwide.

Penguin Family (Spheniscidae)

Common Name *Scientific Name*	Average Length	Weight Range	Size Category
CRESTED GROUP			
Rockhopper *Eudyptes chrysocome*	21½ in (55 cm)	5–10 lb (2.2–4.4 kg)	Lightweight
Fiordland *Eudyptes pachyrhynchus*	21½ in (55 cm)	5½–10¾ lb (2.5–4.9 kg)	Lightweight
Snares *Eudyptes robustus*	22 in (56 cm)	5¾–9½ lb (2.6–4.3 kg)	Lightweight
Erect-crested *Eudyptes sclateri*	26½ in (67 cm)	6½–14 lb (2.9–6.4 kg)	Middleweight
Macaroni *Eudyptes chrysolophus*	27½ in (70 cm)	8–14 lb (3.7–6.4 kg)	Middleweight
Royal *Eudyptes schlegeli*	27½ in (70 cm)	9–18 lb (4.0–8.1 kg)	Middleweight
BANDED GROUP			
Magellanic *Spheniscus magellanicus*	27½ in (70 cm)	8¼–14¼ lb (3.8–6.5 kg)	Middleweight
Humboldt *Spheniscus humboldti*	25½ in (65 cm)	7¾–13 lb (3.6–5.8 kg)	Middleweight
Galápagos *Spheniscus mendiculus*	21 in (53 cm)	3¾–5¾ lb (1.7–2.6 kg)	Featherweight
African or Jackass *Spheniscus demersus*	27½ in (70 cm)	5¼–9 lb (2.4–4.0 kg)	Lightweight
BRUSH-TAILED GROUP			
Adélie *Pygoscelis adeliae*	27½ in (70 cm)	8½–11¾ lb (3.9–5.3 kg)	Middleweight
Chinstrap *Pygoscelis antarctica*	27 in (68 cm)	7½–11 lb (3.4–5.0 kg)	Middleweight
Gentoo *Pygoscelis papua*	31 in (78 cm)	10¼–14¼ lb (4.6–6.5 kg)	Middleweight
LARGE GROUP			
King *Aptenodytes patagonicus*	37½ in (95 cm)	26½–35¼ lb (12–16 kg)	Heavyweight
Emperor *Aptenodytes forsteri*	45 in (115 cm)	55–84 lb (25–38 kg)	Heavyweight
Yellow-eyed *Megadyptes antipodes*	28½ in (72 cm)	9¼–18¾ lb (4.2–8.5 kg)	Middleweight
Little or Fairy *Eudyptula minor*	16½ in (42 cm)	1¾–3 lb (0.8–1.3 kg)	Featherweight

combined height and weight and copied the categories commonly used by professional boxers: featherweight, lightweight, middleweight and heavyweight. Basically, the featherweight and lightweight penguins reach midcalf on a person of average height, the middleweights stand knee-high, the heavyweight king penguin reaches midthigh level, and the heavyweight emperor is almost as tall as the height of the hip joint—which makes the emperor penguin one very big bird.

The last thing I want to mention about the table is the weights, which vary greatly from the smallest species, the little penguin, to the largest, the emperor penguin. An average emperor is twice as heavy as a king penguin, 6 to 9 times heavier than any of the middleweight penguins and 30 times heavier than the featherweight little penguin. The heaviest emperor on record weighed 100 pounds (45 kg), which is considerably more than the weight of some of the female gymnasts in the 1996 Summer Olympics.

The Adélie penguin's long tail identifies it as one of the brush-tailed penguins. All penguins use their tail, in combination with their feet and beak, to steer when they are underwater.

The weight of penguins varies tremendously within a species as well. There are a few reasons for this. First, in all penguin species, the males are slightly heavier than the females, by 10 to 15 percent or so. Weights also vary between the birds from different geographical areas, even different locations on the same island. For example, the birds from one population of gentoo penguins on Îles Kerguélen, in the southern Indian Ocean, weigh an average 12½ pounds (5.7 kg), whereas on the group's 87-mile-long (140 km) Grande Terre, their average weight is just 10 pounds (4.5 kg). Gentoos typically feed close to shore near their colonies, and the body weights of these two penguin populations clearly reflect differences in prey abundance and local oceanographic conditions.

Finally, the weight of an individual bird varies greatly throughout the year. Weight losses of 20 to 35 percent are fairly common when penguins are fasting during courtship and incubation, and during the annual molt, a penguin's body weight may drop by as much as a remarkable 50 percent.

CHAPTER TWO

Penguin Haunts

From the Equator to Antarctica

Although most people associate penguins with the cold, ice and rock of the Antarctic, only seven of the 17 species ever go near this wintry polar region. And only two of these – the Adélie and the emperor – are truly antarctic, that is, penguins which spend their entire lives on the continent or on the pack ice surrounding it. When the first penguins diversified roughly 40 to 50 million years ago, they did so in the southern hemisphere's cool temperate climate, somewhere around 50 degrees south latitude. Today, the largest number of penguin species are still found in these same latitudes, between 45 and 58 degrees south. The greatest diversity – nine species – cohabits the cool waters south of New Zealand (see Appendix 1, page 154).

Clearly, then, penguins are mainly temperate birds, not polar ones. Only later in their evolutionary history did they expand their range to include climates that were more extreme – and extreme they are, indeed. Today, penguins range from the Galápagos Islands, simmering in the glare and swelter of the equatorial sun, south to Cape Royds, an Adélie colony in the Ross Sea at 77 degrees 33 minutes south latitude, deep inside the Antarctic Circle and the most southerly penguin colony of any species. Penguins never made it beyond the southern hemisphere, and it is even quite improbable that one of their kind should roam as far north as the equator. Nevertheless, penguins are not evenly distributed over the vast oceans of the hemisphere. Not all parts of the ocean are equally bountiful, and naturally, the birds live only where there is

Emperor penguins, seen here, and Adélies are the only two penguins that spend their entire lives in the Antarctic. Most penguin species live in more temperate subantarctic regions.

an adequate food supply. A number of areas are particularly rich and productive and determine where most penguins are found.

To begin with, the cold oxygen-charged waters of the Southern Ocean continuously circle Antarctica, flowing in an easterly direction that is driven by the spin of the Earth on its axis. Blocking the path of this great circumpolar current, called the West Wind Drift, are two dozen or so island clusters containing roughly 800 individual islands (see map on page 161). As the current washes past these island groups, it upwells and mixes. When deep water wells to the surface, it carries phosphates, nitrates and silicates with it and spews these nutrients into the sunlit surface waters. The combination of sunlight and nutrients promotes the growth of plankton, the foundation of the entire marine ecosystem. Where plankton is abundant, penguins proliferate.

Upwelling also occurs where the West Wind Drift collides with the southern tips of South America and Africa. Here, part of the current splits off and streams up the western coasts of the two continents. These cold coastal currents, known as the Humboldt Current in South America and the Benguela Current in Africa, are rich in nutrients and support huge populations of seabirds, including three species of penguins.

The Antarctic Convergence is another rich ocean area where penguins concentrate. Here, the cold, dense antarctic waters merge with the warmer, saltier waters of the southern Atlantic, Indian and Pacific oceans along a boundary that completely encircles the antarctic continent. The location of the Convergence meanders between 50 and 60 degrees south latitude and is recognized by most ecologists as the official boundary of the antarctic region, the equivalent of the tree line in the Arctic. Seabird expert Dr. Bryan Nelson describes the Convergence this way: "Where water masses of different properties converge, even in midocean, there is sinking, turbulence and mixing. Often, there is visible and audible evidence of this mixing; the water may be a different color, with whitetops to the breaking waves, hissing and what has been described as the sound of distant surf breaking along a shore."

Taking the Heat and Beating the Chill

As a family, penguins have adapted to the greatest climate range experienced by any group of birds. A Galápagos penguin lives where the water temperature can reach 82°F (28°C) and the

This magellanic penguin has come ashore on a sandy beach in the Falkland Islands, where five penguin species breed.

Gentoo penguins living along the Antarctic Peninsula have shorter beaks and flippers than their northern counterparts. Both adaptations lessen heat loss.

temperature of the feathers on its back in bright sunlight can soar to 124°F (51°C). At the other extreme, the hardy emperor penguin endures winter temperatures as low as minus 76°F (–60°C), winds up to 125 miles per hour (200 km/h) and water near the freezing point year-round. All penguins have roughly the same body temperature, between 100 and 102°F (38°C–39°C). As a result, penguins in the Tropics must frequently rid themselves of surplus body heat to keep from overheating, while those in the Antarctic must constantly guard against the loss of too much body heat in conditions where the air temperature may be up to 180°F (100°C) colder than their blood temperature. How do these remarkable flightless birds take the heat and beat the chill?

If it must, a penguin can always jump into the sea to cool off. Even in the Tropics, the water is generally at least 18°F (10°C) cooler than the bird's body temperature. The consequences of such a simple solution, however, may be serious. For example, one pair of Galápagos penguins that nested in the open had to desert their eggs every day within three hours of sunrise because of the high air temperature. They could not return to incubate until about 4 o'clock in the afternoon, when the day had begun to cool down. Although the birds survived, their eggs were cooked after the first day.

Galápagos penguins guard against such egg losses by nesting in burrows and rock crevices or beneath the protective shade of vegetation, where temperatures are less extreme. This strategy is also employed by the three other banded penguins and the little penguin. But even in these situations, a penguin must often contend with the threat of overheating. It does this in a number of ways. Birds don't have sweat glands, so the penguin can't throw off body heat as a mammal does. Instead, it shunts blood to featherless parts of its body, where heat can be lost more easily. The inside of its mouth, for example, is richly supplied with blood vessels, and a penguin can cool off by panting. All banded penguins also have bare skin on their faces that flushes when the birds warm up. This is another way in which body heat can be lost. The feet and flippers of most penguins account for nearly one-quarter of their entire surface area, so blood shunted to either of these body parts has a large surface area over which to dissipate heat.

At Punta Tomba, Argentina, I watched a group of magellanic penguins return from the sea, hot and winded. Once ashore, the birds stopped to rest and preen. Their flippers were noticeably pink on the underside, and they held them out from their bodies at a 45-degree angle to allow the cooling breeze to circulate around them. The feathers on a penguin's flippers are small, scalelike and less dense than those on its body, which makes it easier for body heat to escape. After 20 minutes or so, the pink flush had faded, and the birds continued inland to their nesting burrows.

For Adélies in Antarctica, 39°F (4°C) may be a heat wave, and even polar penguins occasionally need to cool off. The feet of many penguin chicks are almost adult size when the young birds are just a month old. This may be to help them get rid of surplus body heat. I've watched gentoo chicks suffer from the heat in the Falklands, where temperatures can reach up to 68°F (20°C). On one occasion, I saw dozens of panting chicks sprawled on the ground on their bellies, with their feet and flippers stretched out as far as possible. Lying next to each other, the young penguins looked like so many bloated sunbathers on the French Riviera.

Diving into the cold ocean may be the quickest way for a penguin to chill out, but the bird soon faces another challenge: how to

Temperatures along the coast of Patagonia can climb into the 90s F (30s C). In this kind of heat, nesting magellanic penguins pant to cool off.

keep from cooling down too much. Even the most polar-adapted of the penguins, the emperor, has this problem. When researcher Dr. Gerald Kooyman monitored emperor penguins resting in seawater at a temperature of 29°F (-1.8°C), he noted that the birds "began to shiver after a short time." Kooyman also studied the effects of cold water on Adélie penguins. When the birds were immersed in water at 77°F (25°C), their metabolism rose 1.6 times over what it was when they were resting on land. This increased to 3.5 times when the penguins were dunked in seawater at 41°F (5°C) and climbed to 4.0 times when the water was 29°F (1.8°C), a temperature often encountered by these birds. The metabolic price of doing business in cold water illustrates that although penguins may have in many ways adapted to this environment, they still lose considerable body heat when they are in the water and must replace the energy losses primarily by eating more food.

Penguins at sea may have another way to tip the energy balance—soaking up the warmth of the sun. Researchers have watched African penguins lolling at the ocean's surface in the first two hours after sunrise. Typically, the bird rolls in the water so that one flipper and a foot with the webs spread are held above the surface, where they are exposed to the sun. Similarly, the black feathers on the bird's back, flippers and feet may absorb solar energy and help the penguin warm up after a chilly night at sea. Galápagos penguins have been observed floating high in the water with dry backs. These birds may likewise absorb solar radiation to offset the unavoidable heat losses to the water.

In biology, two trends are noticeable among animals when body heat must be conserved. The first is an increase in body size, and the second is a reduction in the size of the extremities, such as wings, beaks and feet. Both of these characteristics occur in penguins. It's no coincidence that the smallest penguins, the Galápagos and the little penguin, are found in the warmest seas and that the largest one, the emperor, lives year-round in the most polar of latitudes. A large penguin has a smaller surface area relative to its body weight than does a small penguin, so it is better adapted to conserve heat. Although no penguin is truly globular in shape

A downy rockhopper chick tries to beat the heat by extending its flipper and foot to intercept the refreshing breeze drifting off the nearby ocean.

left: Engorged with blood, the flippers of this royal penguin are flushed pink on the underside. By diverting blood to its extremities, a penguin can dissipate body heat when it gets warm.

The Adélie penguin's beak is feathered at the base, both to lessen the body heat the bird loses to the air and to warm the air it breathes.

(a sphere is the optimal shape for heat conservation), the emperor penguin has evolved in that direction. Its surface area is 15 to 30 percent less than is typical for a bird with its body weight.

Relative to other penguin species, emperors have small flippers, beaks and feet. Consider that the average emperor penguin is substantially taller and twice as heavy as its close relative the king penguin, yet its feet, beak and flippers are shorter than those of the king. It's interesting to note that the king penguin is *never* found in latitudes greater than 60 degrees south and that the emperor is *always* found in latitudes greater than 60 degrees, a clear example of habitat partitioning which is based partly on energy costs and returns. Polar penguins employ several other heat-saving devices relating to their beaks and feet. For one, the legs of the emperor penguin are completely feathered and only its toes are bare, while both the legs and the feet of the king penguin are featherless. Another example occurs among the brush-tailed penguins: The beak of the Adélie, the most polar of the three species, is feathered at its base to warm the air it breathes.

Penguins shield themselves from the cold mainly in one way — with feathers. While some of the large penguins may pad their bodies with an inch or so of fat, that fat is primarily an energy reserve rather than a heating blanket. Feathers provide 85 percent of a bird's insulation. The situation is reversed in antarctic seals and whales. These animals rely totally on their fat to insulate them.

Because its feathers are so crucial, a penguin spends considerable time caring for them, as much as three hours each day. Oil is squeezed from the uropygial gland, a nipple-shaped gland at the base of the tail, then spread over the plumage. The oil keeps the feathers supple and water-repellent and also inhibits the growth of fungi and bacteria. A penguin preens both on water and on land, and there is practically no place on its body that it cannot reach. It can even scratch the top of its head by twisting and reaching over its flipper with its foot.

Penguin Impostors

On my first expedition cruise to the Arctic in 1978, there was an elderly Parisian woman on board whose sole reason for making the trip was to catch a glimpse of penguins before she died. Unfortunately, because she was headed north rather than south, it proved to be an impossible dream to realize, but by the end of the cruise, she had transferred her affection to puffins and was able to return home a happy sailor.

Puffins, murres and auklets belong to the auk family (Alcidae) and are the northern-hemisphere look-alikes of the southern hemisphere's penguin family (Spheniscidae). The two groups of birds are similar in many ways. Both the auk and the penguin families have relatively few species. There are just 22 kinds of auks compared with 17 kinds of penguins. Both groups live in cold polar waters,

The king penguin on the right is preening the feathers on its lower back. An oil gland located at the base of its tail enables the bird to spread the oil over its feathers, keeping them waterproof.

The head and beak of the tufted puffin, one of the auks, resemble those of a penguin. Auks fill the same ecological niches in the northern hemisphere that penguins do in the southern hemisphere.

nest in immense colonies, sometimes numbering in the tens of thousands, eat the same food — squid, crustaceans and small fish — and chase their food by "flying" underwater: penguins use their stiff front flippers, while auks use their narrow sickle-shaped wings as though they were flippers. As well, the legs of auks and penguins are positioned near the rear of their bodies, so when on land, the birds stand in an upright position and waddle when they walk. For all these reasons, biologists call auks and penguins ecological equivalents — species that fill the same ecological niche but at opposite ends of the world.

Despite their many similarities, there is one major difference between these birds: auks can fly and penguins cannot. Although auks are able to fly, their wings are relatively small, and they must taxi across the surface of the ocean before finally becoming airborne. Auks are not great flyers for one simple reason: they don't have to be. Auks need to fly just well enough to carry them aloft to steep rocky cliffs and secluded offshore islands, where they breed in crowded, noisy colonies. The birds choose these inaccessible nesting sites to lessen the threat from such predatory land mammals as the brown bear (*Ursus arctos*), the polar bear (*Ursus maritimus*), the wolf (*Canis lupus*) and especially the arctic fox (*Alopex lagopus*). Most penguins do not have such concerns, since there are no native predatory land mammals in Antarctica or on any of the subantarctic islands where the birds nest. This freedom from land predators allows penguin colonies to be horizontal, whereas most auk colonies are vertical.

Although penguins failed to migrate to the northern hemisphere on their own, that didn't stop some enterprising whalers from bringing them here. In August 1936, nine king penguins were released in Norway's Lofoten Islands, above the Arctic Circle. Two years later, an unknown number of penguins were again released in the islands; this time, the penguins were chinstraps and one of the crested penguins, probably macaronis. Some of the transplanted penguins survived in their new home for at least 11 years, but none of them ever bred successfully.

Unfortunately, most of the unwary birds ended their lives rather egregiously. One of the kings was clubbed to death in an "act of mercy, in order to save the bird from its sufferings." The penguin was ashore molting at the time and "looked as though it were ill." Another of the birds drowned when it was accidentally hooked by a fisherman. The fisherman reported that the bird "was fat, and the flesh was tasty." Over the years, three others were shot. One was killed by a farmer's wife when it ventured onto the shore of her property, and another died after its feathers became soiled with oil. The last of the penguins was seen in 1949, when two boys caught a bird that had strayed onto a road near their home. They brought the bird into their kitchen, fed it some cold boiled fish, then carried it down to the beach and released it. The penguin was never seen again.

A flock of thick-billed murres wings over the arctic sea ice, bound for its nesting colony on a nearby cliff. These flying seabirds also use their wings to swim underwater, as do penguins.

CHAPTER THREE

Sex and the Single Penguin

The Breeding Season

Among penguins, the most common breeding pattern is for the birds to assemble at their colonies in late spring, lay their eggs, raise their young in early to midsummer, then fatten and molt in early autumn. After that, they either migrate for the winter or loiter around the colony until the next spring breeding season.

The timing of the breeding cycle in every penguin has evolved over generations and is fine-tuned to coincide with optimal weather conditions, availability of food and, in some cases, a minimum of pressure from predators. Since penguins live in such a diverse range of climates, latitudes and ocean conditions, it's not at all surprising that the timing of the breeding season differs among species. In fact, it would be quite remarkable if the breeding cycle of the Galápagos penguin, which nests on the equator, were the same as that of the emperor, which lives most of its life inside the Antarctic Circle.

Penguins that live in antarctic and subantarctic regions where there is a rich and dependable seasonal food supply generally have a fixed annual cycle, the timing of which follows the example I detailed above. Well over half of all penguins follow this common annual cycle; the others, however, time their breeding cycles differently.

Some of the temperate-latitude penguins start their breeding cycle in the middle of winter, and the chicks finish growing by late spring. This is the pattern followed by fiordland and Humboldt penguins and, in those years when ocean conditions are right, by African and little penguins as well.

A colony of gentoo penguins on Pleneau Island along the Antarctic Peninsula begins its breeding season many weeks later than the gentoos on warmer subantarctic islands.

left: Among chinstrap penguins, experienced dominant birds are able to steal more stones and build larger nests than can subordinate birds.

King penguins returning to their
nesting colony keep their flippers
outstretched to maintain their balance while walking.

The Galápagos penguin lives in the most unpredictable environment of any penguin and has a unique breeding cycle: it may breed during any month of the year and may even breed twice in one year. The breeding cycle of this equatorial penguin is closely tied to the water temperature, which varies from 65 to 82°F (18°C–28°C). When the cold Cromwell Current fails to upwell in the islands, sea temperatures are warm and the penguins do not breed. On average, the penguins breed successfully only when the water temperature is 70°F (21°C) or colder. The colder water temperatures likely encourage a greater growth of plankton, and it is this flush in the food chain that enables the penguins to breed, sometimes twice in a year, if the favorable conditions linger.

Emperors have a breeding pattern unlike that of any other penguin. Emperor penguins cannot begin their breeding cycle in spring, as other antarctic penguins do, because their 9- or 10-month cycle is so long. If the birds were to reproduce in spring, their chicks would hatch in autumn, when food is declining and weather conditions are deteriorating. With such a schedule, few if any emperor chicks would likely survive the winter. As a result, these birds begin their annual cycle in April or May, the austral autumn, when most other antarctic penguins have already left the continent. Adult emperors incubate their eggs at the height of Antarctica's legendary winter, and their chicks then hatch in late winter and grow up during the spring and early-summer months. The young penguins fledge just as the seasonal pulse of food reaches a peak in the Southern Ocean.

The king penguin has the most unusual breeding cycle of all. Like its relative the emperor penguin, the king has a long breeding cycle, but its timing is significantly different. Among kings, adults in a given year are either "early breeders" or "late breeders." Early breeders begin courtship in spring and incubate their eggs through the first part of summer. By the time autumn rolls around, the chicks are three-quarters grown. The large chicks are then left on their own in the colony throughout the winter, where they are typically fed every three or four weeks. In some cases, they are forced to fast for four months or more. Regular feedings begin again the following spring, and at that time, the chicks complete their growth. The king penguin's whole cycle is the longest of any bird, taking from 14 to 16 months.

In the second year, these adult king penguins cannot begin to breed until late summer. As late breeders, they hatch a chick that is still quite small by the start of winter. If the chick survives the

The day after this photograph was taken, a storm struck this Adélie colony on the Antarctic Peninsula, burying the birds under two feet (60 cm) of snow.

winter – and many do not – it does not fledge until the end of the summer. By this time, it is too late in the season for the adults to begin another breeding cycle. As a result, adult kings breed at best just twice in three years. The following spring, the adults begin the three-year cycle all over again, starting off as early breeders. Clearly, the timing of the breeding cycle in penguins varies dramatically among the different species, but in every instance, the pattern adopted is the one that yields the greatest number of offspring.

Truth in Advertising

Roughly one-third of the penguin family are resident species and remain in the area of their colonies throughout the year. These include the African, Humboldt, Galápagos, gentoo, king, yellow-eyed and little penguins. The others are migratory, spending from three to seven months at sea away from their rookeries between breeding seasons. In both cases, however, the fervor of the breeding season fans into flame when the first birds come ashore and begin to prospect for real estate. As adults, almost all penguin species return to the colony in which they themselves hatched. For example, researchers at Cape Adare banded more than 18,000 Adélies, and only 0.3 percent of the birds were ever found nesting anywhere else. Adélie penguins are such homebodies that not only did virtually all of them return to their natal colony to breed, but 77 percent of them eventually bred within 200 yards (180 m) of where they had hatched!

Male penguins usually arrive at the colony a few days to a week ahead of the females, and their first order of business is to find a nest site. Most penguin species nest either on top of the ground, in a shallow open scrape, or in a burrow or rock cavity. King and emperor penguins are the exception. Rather than use a nest, they cradle their single egg on top of their feet. Even so, the king penguin still defends a small plot of turf and guards it against trespassers.

Penguins undoubtedly remember where they nested the year before and frequently use the same site in successive years. In a study on the South Shetland Islands, 63 percent of the male gentoos returned to their previous year's nest, while 94 percent of the chinstraps did the same. The award for faithfulness, however, goes to the male Adélies: 99 percent of them reclaimed the same precious pile of pebbles they had the year before. It's likely that male Adélies are the most faithful of the three species because theirs is

the shortest breeding season, a narrow window of opportunity just three to four months long, and the birds must get started as soon as possible. Another reason for their loyalty is that snow-free ground is at a premium, and if a nest worked once, it's perhaps best not to mess with success.

A male penguin with a nest is only halfway home, however; he also needs a nestmate. Male penguins are not subtle about advertising their ownership of a nest. They scream it out, and the males of every species have their own penetrating trademark call. Anyone who has ever heard a male penguin's ecstatic display would never characterize it as melodious. More common descriptions include grating, raucous, raspy and harsh. The loud trilling call of the yellow-eyed penguin earned it the Maori name *hoiho,* the "noise shouter."

Among Adélie penguins, pebbles are the currency of a colony. Throughout the early breeding season, neighbors steal the stones from each other whenever they can and offer them to their partners.

The orange patches on the neck of a male king penguin are a critical signal used by the bird during courtship. When researchers blackened the patch on one male, he was unable to attract a mate.

British writer A.F. Cobb described the racket at a large colony of rockhoppers: "[It is] as if thousands of wheelbarrows, all badly in need of greasing, are being pushed at full speed." Author Cherry Kearton camped among a colony of African penguins and, after enduring many sleepless nights, wrote: "Imagine yourself in the center of a field in which are tethered a hundred donkeys. And then imagine those donkeys are braying at the same moment." Well, you get the picture. Penguins are big-mouths.

A crooning male of most species is fairly easy to recognize. He stands tall, raises his beak skyward, stretches his neck, opens his mouth and trumpets or brays to the heavens for all he's worth. Some virtuosos beat their flippers rhythmically; the crested species shake their heads rapidly so that their amber locks blur like a golden halo. The call of one vociferous male invariably rouses the guys next door, until a dozen of them are engaged in a heated battle of brays. An outburst may last for over an hour and spread throughout the entire colony.

For many years, the study of animal behavior was dominated by male researchers. This fact undoubtedly had something to do with the bias evident in the interpretation of their subjects' behavior. The old belief was that male animals were the choosy ones. Males competed and sometimes battled with each other, and the winners of such contests then chose the females with which they would mate, typically as many as they could manage. The females, it was assumed, simply had to take what they got.

Times change, and female animals are no longer perceived as the shrinking violets they were once thought to be. The concept of female mate choice is here to stay and is an important component of mate selection in many animal groups, including penguins. Without a doubt, female penguins exercise their gender rights, and indeed, they do the choosing of a mate. But what qualities do they look for in that mate?

The brightly colored feathers on the head of this rockhopper penguin are a visible indicator of the health and vitality of the bird.

Big, colorful males are the choice of most female penguins. The vibrancy of the color on the male's beak, crest or throat patch may reflect his overall health and vigor. When researchers blackened the bright orange ear patches on a male king penguin, the bird not only was unsuccessful in attracting females but failed to evoke even normal aggression from other males.

Females also select males that are large. Such males can probably better defend a nest from interlopers and can drive off thieves that try to steal precious nesting materials. Large males are often fat males, and a male layered with lard is less likely to desert a female's eggs during long incubation stints, when he may be forced to fast for several weeks at a stretch. A fat male may also have other desirable qualities that a female penguin would want passed on to her offspring—namely, the ability to forage well and avoid predators.

Another way in which a female penguin might assess the quality of a male is to listen to his ecstatic display. A large-bodied male brays at a lower frequency and amplitude than its svelte-bodied rivals, and it's possible that the female is able to discern the difference and use the information to help her choose a mate. This kind of information cannot be faked, for it is nature's version of

This rockhopper penguin is incubating on its nest of dried grass. Incubation stints may last up to a week or more.

right: A male magellanic penguin gives an "ecstatic display." The braying noise of the display has earned this bird the common name jackass penguin.

truth in advertising. Adélie penguin researcher Dr. Lloyd Spencer Davis observed: "To female Adélies, a low flat voice is desirable; they don't touch tenors."

Fidelity, Divorce and the Penguin Kiss

After all the posing, parading and caterwauling, roughly 60 to 90 percent of female penguins nonetheless select the same mate they had the previous year. Eighty percent of macaroni pairs, in fact, stay together for at least four successive breeding seasons, and some yellow-eyed penguins may remain together for as long as 13 years. Kings and emperors, however, show the least fidelity to former mates. Only 29 percent of kings pair up again, and just 15 percent of emperors do so. The staggered breeding cycles of kings may make it more difficult for pairs to coordinate their rendezvous at the colonies, but the reason emperors show such low mate fidelity is still unclear. Researcher Dr. Tony Williams observed that penguin species which spend more time together at the nest are more likely to remate in subsequent years. Emperor and king pairs spend the least amount of time associating with each other during the breeding season, which may explain why they are less inclined to stay together from one season to the next.

Penguin pairs may fail to remate for a number of reasons. One of the penguins may die during the winter or be killed by a leopard seal (*Hydrurga leptonyx*) or a killer whale (*Orcinus orca*). A partner may simply not show up, thereby skipping a breeding season. Sometimes, both partners return on time, but one of them chooses a different mate.

Yes, penguins divorce each other, and in some species, the divorce rate may climb to 13 percent, which of course is still much lower than the 50 percent rate for human marriages in North America. It seems that penguins divorce for some of the same reasons humans do, and one of these is incompatibility. In penguin terms, this means a pair may fail to synchronize behaviors to the extent required to undertake the complicated scheduling involved in incubating the eggs, brooding and provisioning the chicks. For example, if one partner delays its return to the nest, the other one may be forced to desert the eggs or the chicks may starve. In either case, the breeding season is lost. As a result, one of the

These royal penguins were squabbling at the water's edge at the end of a foraging period at sea. It was not clear why they were fighting.

unsuccessful pair often selects another mate the following year.

At the start of the breeding season, things may really heat up when a male penguin, fat and full of fight, returns and finds his old nest occupied by another male — or worse, the squatter has usurped both his old nest and his former partner. Then the feathers fly. Rival penguins bump chests, grip, growl, wrestle with their sharp-edged beaks and beat each other with their stiff flippers. Fights may last for more than 15 minutes, but such prolonged bouts usually occur only when the two males have a strong claim to the same mate or nesting site.

Seabird expert Robert Cushman Murphy was ringside on many occasions when male Adélies clashed: "Rival cocks may begin a battle with their beaks, but they soon resort entirely to blows of the flippers and end by leaning against each other in a sidewise position, battering away with the outside wings like clenched pugilists raining blows until the battering sounds like a tattoo. Although blood is frequently drawn during such battles, serious injuries are rare, and the end of a combat usually comes when one of the pair is out of breath."

Cherry Kearton watched a truculent male African penguin trundle home to his burrow only to discover that a trespasser had moved in with his mate while he was temporarily away at sea. A six-hour struggle ensued before the trespasser was finally evicted. "He was certainly in a very bad way," wrote Kearton. "From his neck three-quarters of the way to his feet, his feathers were literally soaked in blood. His head was quite dreadful to look at — raw with open wounds. And both his eyes were so battered as to be practically sightless."

Male penguins are not the only fighters. Females also tear into each other, especially when one of them discovers that her former partner has moved in with a new mate. The female reaction to such a penguin predicament is simple: Drive out the new femme fatale and settle down with your old partner, even if he has been unfaithful.

In human terms, it seems that penguins readily forgive and forget, and both the male and the female in a pair will overlook the occasional dalliance. For example, if a female Adélie returns to her old nest and her partner is not there, she will pair with the nearest

unattached male neighbor. If her old mate shows up within the next seven days, she will promptly abandon her new partner for the old one. If her former mate arrives more than a week late, he's out of luck, and the female remains with her new partner. Male Adélies are just as flexible. If his partner fails to appear, the male will court any and every eligible female that wanders near him until one of them finally stays. If his old mate suddenly reappears, the male stands back and lets the females flail it out, then welcomes the victor with open flippers. What matters in the end is whether the pair has successfully raised chicks before; if it has, the two are likely to pair again.

Wherever there are winners, there must be losers, and penguins are no exception. Not all the birds that amble ashore at a colony are successful in claiming a nest and attracting a mate. In some cases, it may take many seasons for this to happen. To begin

Kings have one of the highest divorce rates among penguins — roughly three-quarters of them mate with a different partner each season.

Breeding penguins tenaciously occupy their nest territory even in the worst weather conditions. This mud-covered gentoo refused to leave its nest despite high winds and heavy rain.

with, every young penguin needs at least two or three years at sea practicing and perfecting its fishing skills before it can attempt to breed. There are a couple of reasons for this. Among the migratory species, a prospective breeder may face a long journey across sea ice simply to reach the colony. It may have to fast while it is traveling, and that can be accomplished successfully only if the bird is proficient enough at feeding itself to build up the necessary fat reserves. The young bird needs to be in prime physical condition for another reason. Predatory seals and sea lions lurk around many penguin rookeries, and avoiding these hazards requires strength, stamina and accomplished swimming skills.

The first year a young penguin visits a breeding colony, it usually arrives fairly late in the season, often not until December or January. Each year after that, it arrives a little bit earlier. These inexperienced birds typically spend a year or two as "wanderers," trudging around the colony, usually near the site where they hatched—an area with which they are familiar. Remember that three-quarters of all Adélies eventually nest within 200 yards (180 m) of where they grew up.

Even when young penguins finally arrive at a colony pudgy, punctual and in their sexual prime, many of them still fail to breed. It might be that even though the birds are physically ready to mate, they are still socially inept. Jazz pianist Duke Ellington described their situation best with the immortal words: "It don't mean a thing if you ain't got that swing." In young penguins, courtship behavior and aggression are often confused. An inexperienced male penguin may mistakenly threaten a potential mate, even attack her. Clearly, such behavior is not conducive to successful pair formation. Basically, territorial male penguins need to overcome their natural tendency to attack strangers, and unattached females need to overcome their innate reluctance to approach males. In the same way that young birds must practice swimming and fishing skills before they can breed successfully, they must also polish their social behavior. In all likelihood, they do this by playing out their courtship routine on a succession of prospective mates and learning from their failures—failures that may well span a number of seasons.

The females in most penguin species breed for the first time when they are 3 or 4 years old, a year or two sooner than their male counterparts. The largest species, the kings and emperors, take a little longer to mature and usually start breeding when they are 6 years of age. As a group, the crested penguins take the longest to get into the swing of things. Commonly, they are 5 or 6 before they begin breeding, and some macaroni and royal penguins may not begin until they are 7 to 9 years old.

Once two penguins settle down together, they begin the task of building a bond, the strength of which may determine whether they successfully rear chicks or not. Within the penguin family, each species has its own repertoire of displays and calls to achieve this and to bring the birds into synchrony. Typically, courting birds try to be as unintimidating as they can by hiding their bills, exposing vulnerable parts of their body and using appeasement displays such as bowing. Courting penguins also sing duets, although it's probably stretching it to call these mutual displays singing. They

A male chinstrap penguin vocalizes at the start of an "ecstatic display." Such displays are a way for the male to advertise his vigor, as well as his ownership of a nesting territory, to prospective mates.

Rockhopper penguins preen each other in a courtship display. Mutual care is a way for birds to reinforce their bond and to remove external parasites.

can certainly be described as duets, however, delivered with all the enthusiasm that unbridled sexual hormones can arouse. The cacophony of wheezing rattles rising from a large macaroni colony where the pairs are in full voice can be truly deafening.

Some pairs also nibble and preen the feathers on each other's head and neck. This delicate courtship behavior probably evolved initially as a way for pairs to reduce external parasites and only later became part of the behavioral cement that bonds them. Such mutual preening is seen primarily in temperate and equatorial penguin species. These birds are frequently heavily infested with fleas and ticks. One little penguin examined was peppered with 187 bloodsucking ticks. Most ticks drop off and desiccate when a penguin goes to sea, but when a bird is molting or incubating and its mate is not around to preen it, the troublesome tumescent ticks triumph. Penguins that breed in cold regions—emperors,

Adélies, gentoos and chinstraps — are not plagued by these creatures, so mutual preening is not part of their courtship repertoire.

Between the purring and the petting, penguin pairs renovate. Burrows are padded with grass, seaweed and sticks. Surface nests are dusted out, and the pebbles, twigs, bones and feathers rearranged. This is especially entertaining to watch, because penguins are incurable kleptomaniacs. One early penguin researcher painted pebbles bright red and left a pile of them near a nest-covered knoll of Adélies. Within hours, the stone-stealing started. After three days, the red pebbles had been looted from one nest to the next and carried throughout the colony.

In their thievery, penguins are shameless, and no other bird can pilfer with such panache. In 1898, Louis Bernacchi, a young Australian physicist, observed the behavior with amusement: "The thief slowly approaches the one he wishes to rob with a most creditable air of nonchalance and disinterestedness, and if, on getting close, the other looks at him suspiciously, he will immediately gaze around almost childlike and bland and appear to be admiring the scenery. The assumption of innocence is perfect; but no sooner does the other look in a different direction than he will dart down on one of the pebbles of its nest and scamper away with it in his beak."

Eventually, the feathered foreplay culminates in copulation. When you are shaped like a football, that's harder to do than it sounds. After watching several pairs of rockhoppers mate, I recorded these observations in my journal:

"Once the female is sprawled invitingly on her belly, the male hops up onto her back and slowly treads backward. A mounted male reminds me of an excited youngster trying to balance on a skateboard. The enthusiastic suitor nibbles the feathers on his partner's crown and neck, wags his tail from side to side and slaps her flanks with his flippers like a cowboy urging his horse on. As I sit here watching the penguins procreate, the pairs that have mated are easy to spot. It has been raining for the last couple of days, and all the females have muddy tread marks on their backs.

"Penguins have no penis, so once the male is in the hit zone, the pair simply pucker and pout their cloacae and exchange a wet

In penguins, the act of mating is something of a balancing act. The male king pictured here fell off his partner twice before finally achieving his goal.

kiss with their bottoms. In an instant—actually three or four seconds—millions of sperm are headed upstream. The whole affair takes just about a minute. Afterward, the birds sometimes preen and coo to each other and then collect more nesting material. It reminds me of a married couple I once knew who had a regular weekend routine: midmorning sex, then the fellow would go out and mow the lawn."

A penguin pair may start to copulate several weeks before the first egg is laid, and as the time of laying draws closer, the birds may mount as often as 12 to 14 times a day. Many copulations, however, are thwarted by bystanders. In most cases, the meddlesome spectators are unattached males or mated males from a neighboring nest. Eventually, however, the eggs arrive, and the singles scene is over for the penguins. After that, the chores of family life begin: fasting, frantic feeding and continually topping up the chirping chicks.

Crowd-Crazy Colonies

At the turn of the century, naturalist Dr. Edward Wilson penned this colorful description of an Adélie colony at Cape Adare, in the Ross Sea in Antarctica: "Such a sight….[Penguins] covered the plain, which was nearly 200 acres [80 ha] in extent….The place was the color of anchovy paste from the excreta of the young penguins. It simply stunk like hell, and the noise was deafening. There was a series of stinking, foul stagnant pools full of green scum, and the rest of the plain was literally covered with guano. And bang in the center of this horrid place was our camp."

Since sex is the single biggest event in a penguin's life, what you also see in a penguin colony are sex-driven individuals with three overriding thoughts: sex, sex, sex. Penguins are not shy about sex. They are enthusiastic voyeurs and blatant exhibitionists, and as with virtually every other activity in their lives, they prefer to do it as a group.

As I've observed, penguins are creatures of habit, and they use the same traditional colonies year after year. After visiting the huge magellanic penguin colony at Punta Tomba, Argentina, bird artist Roger Tory Peterson wrote: "The ground in which magellanics dig their burrows is like an ancient graveyard. The fragmentary remains of hundreds of generations are buried deep under the pebbles, earth and drifting sand. Some colony sites almost certainly go

The spacing between birds in a chinstrap colony is fairly constant: The birds position themselves just out of pecking range from one another.

back thousands of years and can claim a greater antiquity, a longer history of occupancy, than any human city."

Peterson was mistaken about the age of the Punta Tomba colony, which is now estimated to be no more than 114 years old. But he was right in predicting that some penguin colonies can be very, very old. Indeed, carbon-14 dating of an Adélie colony in Antarctica confirms that some traditional breeding sites may have been occupied since they first became free of ice at the end of the last glaciation, possibly 4,000 to 5,000 years ago.

Most penguin colonies are situated on level or slightly sloping ground, but the approaches to the nesting sites vary considerably. For example, gentoos nesting on the Falkland Islands often have flat sandy beaches on which to land but then may have to trek almost two miles (3 km) inland to reach their colony. The daredevil crested penguins frequently seem to select rocky coastlines, where the surge is violent or where thick, tangled belts of giant kelp separate the birds from the security of shore. Nor is their work over once they reach shore. Some macaronis on South Georgia must climb for an hour and a half to reach their crowded rookery.

Macaronis aren't the only penguin alpinists. Chinstraps on Deception Island ford rushing meltwater streams, then struggle up steep slopes of volcanic ash as high as 1,600 feet (500 m) above sea level to reach their lofty colony, which is often shrouded in clouds.

Such hardships seem trivial, however, when compared with the journeys made by Adélies and emperors returning to their colonies. When many Adélies arrive at their rookeries in early October, the frigid grip of late winter still clutches much of Antarctica, and the birds may have to cross expanses of sea ice up to 50 miles (80 km) wide before they reach land. Emperors may tread and toboggan a remarkable 125 miles (200 km) to reach their colonies.

An Adélie colony on Paulet Island was the first really large penguin colony I ever saw. I wrote this description in my journal: "The racket, the acrid odor and the bustle of bodies assailed my senses in a delicious wave. Penguins stretched from headland to headland and to the tops of many of the black volcanic slopes. The scene was strangely primordial, as though I were glimpsing the beginning of time, the birth of being. The pulse of unbridled Nature was almost palpable. Never have I seen such a concentrated profusion of life."

Ninety-five percent of all seabirds breed in colonies, and penguins do it on as grand a scale as any. Imagine 19,000 pairs of big-bodied emperors huddled together on the sea ice at Cape Washington or 55,000 pairs of kings at Lusitania Bay, on

Numbering roughly 10 million, macaroni penguins are the most abundant penguins in the world. Nearly half of the birds nest on South Georgia, as do the macaronis shown here.

Macquarie Island. The brush-tailed penguins can crowd together in even greater densities: 100,000 pairs of braying chinstraps nest at Bailey Head, on Deception Island, and an incomprehensible 272,000 pairs of Adélies crowd the slopes of Cape Adare, on the ice-choked coast of Antarctica.

Of course, not all penguin colonies are large. Gentoos often breed in groups of fewer than 1,000 birds, and every species, except the emperor, has small splinter colonies of a couple of dozen birds or fewer. There's an interesting explanation as to why emperor colonies seldom contain fewer than several hundred pairs: This may be the critical minimum number of penguins that must huddle together to offset the drain of body heat the birds experience during the many cold months of winter.

Although penguin colonies vary dramatically in size, the birds nest close together even when there is space for them to spread out, and the spacing is fairly predictable from species to species. The yellow-eyed penguin is the least social member of the family. Yellow-eyes don't seem to mind *listening* to their neighbors, but they don't want to *see* them. In fact, if two nesting pairs can see each other, one or both of the pairs will abandon the nest. As a result, yellow-eyes commonly nest in thick underbrush, where the visibility is restricted and nests can be up to 165 yards (150 m) apart.

The burrow-nesting banded penguins are much more tolerant of one another. Little penguins usually dig their nest holes at least 6½ feet (2 m) apart, and African and magellanic penguins may honeycomb a colony, with a burrow occupying every square yard. The brush-tailed penguins are just as sociable, and the density of their colonies varies between 0.3 and 1.4 nests per square yard. Of these, Adélies crowd together the most and gentoos the least, but all of them are at least pecking distance apart.

The differences in the density of colonies among the brush-tailed group are partially a reflection of the amount of nesting habitat available to the birds. Virtually the entire Adélie world population of 2.5 million pairs nests on the antarctic continent and its nearby islands. There, less than 2 percent of the land is free of ice at the height of summer, and nesting habitat is consequently limited. Most chinstraps and gentoos nest farther north than do Adélies, so their colonies tend to be much less cramped. Northern gentoos nesting on Îles Crozet are virtual land barons, with each pair claiming 24 square yards (20 m²) of nesting space, while gentoos on the crowded Antarctic Peninsula must cram eight nests into the same area.

Crested penguins, especially rockhoppers, royals and macaronis, really squeeze together, with as many as 2.4 pairs sharing every square yard. The nests may be just 24 inches (60 cm) apart, which is not far when your neighbor is a two-foot-tall (60 cm) bad-tempered bully wielding a menacing beak.

Of all the penguins, the emperors crowd together the most. They are the only penguins that do not defend a nesting territory. The adults simply shuffle around with a single egg balanced on the top of their feet, keeping it warm with a feathered fold of belly skin. In very cold weather, emperors may bunch together 10 to the square yard, with individuals resting their beaks on the shoulders of the birds in front of them.

Crowd-crazy penguins may nest with groups of other seabirds as well. On New Zealand's Bounty Islands, I photographed erect-crested penguins nesting side by side with one of the mollymawks, the shy albatross (*Diomedea cauta*); in the Falklands, rockhoppers

The face of a Humboldt penguin has large areas of bare skin through which the bird can dissipate body heat.

Nearly full-grown, the downy brown king penguin chicks clustered in groups throughout this huge colony on Salisbury Plain on South Georgia are as large as the adults.

and imperial cormorants (*Phalacrocorax atriceps*) frequently share the same turf; and little penguins of Australia sometimes occupy burrows next to those of the short-tailed shearwater (*Puffinus tenuirostris*).

Colony nesting is so common among penguins and other seabirds that there must be some benefits to be derived from this behavior. Researchers often suggest that penguins squeeze together because there are a limited number of nesting sites. Although that may be the case for several species, such as the Adélies, there are other important reasons penguins like to crowd and cram.

Information sharing is one of the benefits. When food is scattered and its location unpredictable, as krill and shoaling fish commonly are, a few penguins searching separately may easily miss such prey. When an entire colony of penguins is foraging over a large area, however, there is a much better chance that at least some of the birds will discover where the krill and fish are concentrated. Once they have done so, other members of the colony can follow these birds to the food source.

Large groups of penguins are also more effective at detecting the approach of predatory birds, such as skuas or caracaras, then fighting them off. A few penguins out on their own are less successful at doing this.

Finally, groups of penguins seem better able to synchronize their breeding behavior, and the flurry of courtship calls and displays probably helps an individual bird come into final reproductive condition. A colony in which most penguins are incubating quietly at the same time or are preoccupied with the busy task of feeding hungry chicks is a much safer place for eggs and young than a disruptive assemblage of pairs all doing something different.

As a species, penguins enjoy yet another benefit to synchronization. When the majority of chicks hatch at roughly the same time, the predators in the area are saturated with potential prey. That reduces the total number of chicks the predators can kill and also lessens the chances that any particular individual penguin chick will fall victim.

CHAPTER FOUR

Family Life

An incubating gentoo penguin shifts its feet. The eggshells of penguins are exceptionally thick, thus preventing accidental breakage by clumsy adults.

Egg-Citing Details

Like most seabirds, penguins lay small clutches of eggs. The largest penguins, kings and emperors, lay a single egg, while all the others lay a pair of eggs. Compare this with the records of a few land birds, some of which are prodigious layers. One European blue tit (*Parus caeruleus*), the size of a chickadee, laid 22 eggs, and a northern bobwhite quail (*Colinus virginianus*) from the southeastern United States laid 28 eggs. When a curious biologist repeatedly removed eggs from the nest of a northern flicker (*Colaptes auratus*), a common woodpecker of North America, the persevering bird was persuaded to lay 71 eggs in just 73 days.

Penguins, however, have a very limited capacity to lay extra eggs. Little penguins can sometimes lay a replacement clutch if the first pair of eggs is lost, and some Adélies can lay a third egg if one of theirs is snatched by a predator, but this is an uncommon trait in penguins. When a penguin loses its eggs, it typically must wait until the next breeding season to try again. The explanation for these low egg-laying rates is straightforward. Because penguins forage far from the nest, feeding frequency is low. The parents are therefore unable to provide for more than one or two chicks at one time.

Penguin eggs are also smaller in relation to the female's body weight than in almost any other group of birds. According to the *1995 Guinness Book of Animal Records,* the single egg of an emperor penguin weighs just 1.4 percent of the female's body weight, the smallest for any bird. The record at the other extreme belongs to the brown kiwi (*Apteryx australis*), a New Zealand bird about the size of a chicken that lays one or two huge eggs, each of which weighs roughly 25 percent of the female's weight. Ouch!

left: The king penguin, shown here, and the emperor penguin each lay a single egg and balance it on top of their feet during the incubation period.

Although the egg of an emperor penguin is proportionally small, the egg of any 65-pound (30 kg) bird is still likely to be pretty big. In one study, emperor eggs weighed an average 15½ ounces (438 g). Such an egg would whip up into an eight-chicken-egg omelet, but depending upon what the bird had been eating beforehand, the omelet might not look so appetizing. Penguins that have eaten fish or squid usually lay eggs with familiar yellow yolks. However, if the bird has eaten krill, the yolk may be a startling bright crimson. For this reason, early settlers on the Falkland Islands sometimes called the rockhopper the red penguin.

All freshly laid penguin eggs are dull white in color and tinged with pale green or pale blue. In the grunge and guano of a penguin colony, the eggs soon become heavily stained. Kicked and rolled around as they are, often on sharp rocks, penguin eggs must have strong shells, and indeed, they do. South African seabird researcher A.J. Williams observed that the heaviest eggshells among seabirds belong to penguins, cormorants and murres, all of which have legs positioned at the rear of their bodies and are, as a result, less agile when walking. Williams speculated that the birds' clumsiness at the nest leads to an increased loss of eggs; thick eggshells evolved as a response to this.

Fifteen of the seventeen species of penguins lay two eggs, and in the majority of these, both eggs are roughly the same size. The exceptions are the six crested penguins. In these birds, the first egg is between 15 and 40 percent smaller than the second one, and although the birds always lay two eggs, they virtually never raise two chicks. But if just one chick survives, why lay two eggs in the first place and why make the first egg so small?

For decades, penguin experts have discussed and speculated about the reasons for this behavior, and there is still no completely satisfactory explanation. Here is what is known. The degree of size difference among the eggs of the six crested species seems to correlate with the degree of crowding in the colony and the aggression level of the males, especially early in the nesting season, when male belligerence is highest. For example, fiordland penguins are the most widely spaced of the crested penguins and show the least difference in the size of their eggs. Macaroni and royal penguins are at the other end of the scale. They live in the most crowded colonies, neighboring birds are extremely aggressive with one another, and the eggs of these penguins are the most dissimilar in size. After a visit to Macquarie Island, I described the fate of some eggs in a colony of royal penguins: "The male adversaries locked beaks and, with

A male rockhopper penguin, identifiable by its deeper, heavier beak, incubates a single egg, while its partner stands nearby. A week earlier, the pair had had two eggs.

The chirping chick inside this rockhopper penguin egg was ignored by the adult, which was already brooding a small downy youngster. By the end of the day, the unhatched chick had chilled and died.

their flippers flailing, fought their way across nearly 10 yards [9 m] of the crowded colony. In the fever of the fight, they blundered over the backs of other birds guarding their eggs. The combatants seemed oblivious to the rattling screams, vicious pecks and flipper blows from the owners of those territories they accidentally invaded. When it was over, one egg was broken and another displaced from its nest."

The small first egg in the crested penguins seems quite expendable and may simply be the price the birds pay for their extreme aggressiveness. In any case, in the majority of royal penguins, if the puny first egg is not crushed or punctured during a fight early in the nesting season, it is actively kicked out of the nest by one of the adult birds, usually shortly after the second egg is laid. If that's all there is to it, why don't the birds simply wait until the worst of the territorial squabbling is over and lay a single large egg? The situation is undoubtedly far more complex than this, and the debate over the little egg continues.

No bird incubates its eggs internally, as mammals do, so the eggs of a bird must be warmed externally and kept as close to body temperature as possible. To do this, penguins, and most other birds, have areas of bare vascularized skin on their lower bellies that they press against the top of their eggs. Without such featherless areas, known as brood patches, penguins could never warm the eggs sufficiently, because their feathers, which normally insulate the birds so well, would prevent the transfer of any body heat. The feathers are lost from the brood-patch area at the start of the breeding season and begin to regrow again shortly after the eggs hatch.

The normal development of an egg requires not only warmth but turning as well. The top of a king penguin's egg resting against the bird's brood patch is 9 to 13°F (5–7°C) warmer than the bottom of the egg cradled on the penguin's feet. This is one reason the birds turn their eggs regularly. Turning also keeps the membranes within the egg from adhering to the inside of the shell and interfering with the normal growth of the embryo.

The incubation period — the time during which the egg is heated by an adult — varies with the size of the penguin. In the little penguin, it lasts roughly 33 days; in the medium-sized species, it varies between 35 and 40 days; and it is longest in the two largest species.

King penguins incubate for 54 to 56 days, while the emperor cradles its single egg for 64 days. The great albatrosses and the kiwis incubate their eggs for a longer time, 71 to 84 days, but they leave their nests at intervals to feed, so the emperor holds the record for the longest continuous incubation.

In all species of penguins, with the exception of the emperor, both sexes share in the incubation of the eggs, but the duty roster differs among the species. In gentoo, yellow-eyed and magellanic penguins, for example, the mates alternate frequently, usually relieving each other every one to three days. In chinstraps and all the crested penguins, each sex typically starts with a long incubation shift lasting between 7 and 14 days, after which the partners change over more frequently as the time of hatching gets closer. In Adélies, the first incubation stint, which is always taken by the male, may take even longer, up to three weeks. In years when the sea ice melts late, it may take that long for a female Adélie to journey to open water and back again. In one case, a female traveled 210 miles (340 km), and in another instance, 150 miles (240 km), sometimes swimming against strong ocean currents and tobogganing and walking for a week over the sea ice to return to her mate. By the end of his vigil, the incubating male Adélie may have been ashore fasting for

Each of these adult emperor penguins has a partner guarding a chick back at the breeding colony. These birds are heading out to sea on a foraging trip.

as long as six weeks and lost 40 percent of his body weight. If the female takes too long to return, the male will have no choice but to desert the eggs; his alternative is starvation.

The incubation travails of all other species pale, however, when compared with those of the male emperor penguin, which ranks as one of the most remarkable feats in the natural world. The female emperor lays her egg in May, passes it to her mate and then promptly trundles back to the sea, leaving the male to face the raw edge of winter and parenting alone. Some Father's Day gift! The male emperor carries the egg for the full incubation period, enduring blizzard after blizzard in continuous polar darkness, fasting for 15 weeks or more and losing half of his body weight, and still he tenaciously cradles the precious egg.

Veteran British researcher Dr. Bernard Stonehouse watched incubating male emperors achieve these "extraordinary acrobatic feats": "Scratching the back of the head with the claws of one foot while balancing and holding the egg firmly on the other was seen on a number of occasions. Again, a bird holding an egg was seen to cross a nine-inch-wide [23 cm] crack in the ice by falling bodily across and dragging itself forward with beak and flippers. Similarly, birds have been known to fall over small precipices, roll down snowy slopes, trip over rocks, tumble heavily on slippery bare ice or navigate their way among very rough sastrugi [wind-packed snowdrifts] without releasing their grip on the eggs."

Possibly the greatest feat of the male emperor is simply to survive the antarctic winter. Emperors meet this challenge by huddling together on the exposed surface of the sea ice. By packing in tight groups, 8 to 10 per square yard (0.8 m²), an individual emperor reduces the surface area of its body that is exposed to the heat-stealing wind and cold. This translates into astonishing energy savings. A bird on its own can lose up to 0.66 pounds (0.3 kg) of body weight in a day. When an individual is crowded into a huddle, this drops to as little as 0.26 pounds (0.12 kg), a 150 percent energy saving without which the birds could never endure their lengthy winter fasts.

During storms, the birds in these huddles shift positions continuously. Those on the exposed windward side of a group slowly shuffle along the outside edges until they find shelter in the lee of the cluster, where they subsequently become surrounded by new arrivals. Thus every bird takes its turn shielding its companions. A shifting huddle such as this may creep several hundred yards over the flat surface of the sea ice during a storm. Imaginative French

researchers call these slow-moving clusters of males, sometimes numbering 5,000 strong, *tortues,* or turtles.

The urge to incubate can be very strong, especially, it seems, in emperor and king penguins. Stonehouse observed that emperors which lose an egg "will readily take up an extraordinary variety of substitute objects, ranging from a brown leather camera case to dead fish, so long as the object was a suitable size and portable; the shape and color seemed immaterial."

Incubating kings seem no more discriminating. Stonehouse watched a hopeful king penguin on South Georgia sit for three days with a cylindrical tin six inches (15 cm) long and three inches (7.5 cm) in diameter sticking out from beneath its belly fold "like a ventilating shaft." More understandable is the use of substitutes by captive penguins. Kings at the Edinburgh Zoo in Scotland have cradled egg-shaped stones, bottles, tins and even a stale dinner bun.

A pair of Adélie penguins greet each other in a loud vociferous "mutual display." The bird in the rear is relieving its incubating mate after an incubation shift that can last for several weeks.

The brood patch in penguins is a featherless area on the bird's belly, as shown in this chinstrap. The highly vascularized skin in the brood patch keeps the egg within a few degrees of the bird's body temperature.

The relief of an incubating penguin by its mate is never a quiet affair. Penguins recognize each other by their voices, but sometimes, just the sight of a partner may be enough to start an intense greeting ceremony in which the birds bray or trumpet in unison. Once you've watched a pair of macaronis reunite, it's hard to imagine greater enthusiasm or noise. After the incubating bird has been sitting for some time, it usually looks bedraggled and smeared with mud and guano, in sharp contrast to its sleek, clean-looking mate. When the birds have seemingly howled themselves hoarse, it's usually only a matter of minutes before they swap places and the newcomer settles on the eggs. Even though in some cases, the off-duty bird may not have eaten for weeks, it may still loiter around the nest. Often, it will preen its mate, reinforcing the bond between them, then gather—or more likely pilfer—some pebbles or other materials, adding them ceremoniously to the nest before it finally departs for the sea.

In 1995, a trio of Spanish researchers reported some interesting observations about nest relief and stone stealing in chinstraps breeding on Deception Island, in the South Shetland Islands. The researchers discovered that male chinstraps collected larger stones, wandered farther afield to do so and stole more stones than did their female partners. The nests of some pairs tripled in weight during the incubation and brooding periods, sometimes weighing in at 23 pounds (10.5 kg) and containing up to 641 stones. Other nests shrank by as much as 70 percent. The biologists concluded that dominant males built the largest nests and defended them best. Subordinate males, on the other hand, were neither able to defend their nests nor able to collect enough stones to offset theft by their neighbors.

Chinstraps are not the only penguins to build large nests. In 1921, 19-year-old Thomas Bagshawe was marooned with a companion on the Antarctic Peninsula for 10 months over the winter. During his ordeal, this tenacious young man refused to let his spirit be broken, and he kept busy collecting scientific data, including details on the composition of gentoo penguin nests. One nest examined by Bagshawe contained 1,700 pebbles and 70 old tail feathers.

With all the thievery that goes on in a penguin colony, do large nests confer any advantage to the nest owner? The answer is a resounding yes. In the South Shetland Islands in the 1990s, nearly one-third of the chinstrap nests being studied flooded with meltwater after a snowstorm, and in over half of those, the eggs washed away or the hatchlings drowned. The researchers observed that the

flooded nests were significantly smaller than the ones which with-stood the storm and concluded that stone theft in chinstraps improves nest quality and thereby enhances reproductive success.

Adélie nests can also flood with meltwater, and stone scrounging can save the day for these nests as well. During a thaw on Signy Island, in the South Orkneys, biologist Dr. William Sladen watched and recorded the fate of an Adélie nest with a stream of ice-cold water pouring through it: "The lone incubating male, his eggs half submerged, was collecting and arranging stones around himself. Next day, the eggs were above water level and dry, though the stream still passed on either side of the nest. The eggs eventually hatched."

Bad weather can cause a major loss of eggs. Strong, gusting winds can blow eggs right out of a shallow penguin nest. One year, Sladen reported that nearly 90 percent of the eggs from a large colony of Adélies at Hope Bay, in Antarctica, were lost when the

A cluster of southern elephant seal bachelors lounges on a beach on the Falkland Islands. If these huge seals accidentally lumber through a colony of nesting penguins, the results can be disastrous.

colony was battered by repeated storms. Snowstorms can also imprison an incubating bird and bury it so that only its head shows through a hole in the hard-packed snow. If a bird is buried like this for more than a few consecutive days, it usually deserts the eggs.

Eggs that aren't frozen, flooded, blown away or deserted may still fail to hatch. In every penguin species, a percentage of the eggs, sometimes as many as one-quarter of them, are infertile, especially those of first-time breeders. Eggs can also get punctured by an errant toenail and addle. Dutiful parents have been known to brood such rotten eggs for a month beyond the normal hatching time. Probably one of the most unusual causes of egg loss is trampling by elephants—the southern elephant seal (*Mirounga leonina*), that is. These five-ton (4,500 kg) blubbery beasts share the same landing beaches as magellanics, royals, gentoos and kings on many islands in the sub-Antarctic. When the penguins happen to nest on flat ground near the beach, these behemoths can lumber through a colony, scattering the adults and crushing innumerable eggs.

Eggnappers and Ice Borers

Wherever there are eggs, there are certain to be eggnappers, and every penguin colony has its share of these. In the Galápagos Islands, the unlikely culprits are crimson-shelled Sally lightfoot crabs (*Grapsus grapsus*) and Galápagos snakes (*Philodryas biserialis*); in Australia, there are blue-tongued lizards (*Tiliqua* spp) and deadly venomous tiger snakes (*Notechis scutatus*); in Africa, mongooses and sacred ibises (*Threskiornis aethiopicus*); and in Argentina, Geoffroy's cats (*Felis geoffroyi*) and furtive gray foxes (*Dusicyon griseus*). On many islands where sealers clubbed and butchered their victims, the pets of these soft-hearted souls went wild and ravaged the resident nesting seabirds, which were unaccustomed to predators. Today, a mix of introduced rats, escaped ferrets and stoats and feral dogs and cats eat penguin eggs in Australia and New Zealand and in many of the subantarctic islands south of them.

Two of the most conspicuous egg robbers are sheathbills and skuas, birds whose tactics are notorious among penguin watchers. The pale-faced sheathbill, with its scaly, warty visage, is currently my favorite bird to photograph in the antarctic region. I've always had a strange attraction to the so-called uglies of the natural world. First, I became intrigued by wrinkle-headed vultures squabbling over a bloated, fetid carcass. Then I was drawn to lumpy-faced

warthogs rooting in mud and filth. After that, my attention was captured by slime-coated snapping turtles lurking in bug-infested swamps. Now I'm hooked on sheathbills, birds with a lifestyle to suit their lack of good looks.

There are two species of sheathbill: the pale-faced sheathbill (*Chionis alba*), which lives in the South Atlantic and adjacent Antarctic Peninsula, and the black-faced sheathbill (*C. minor*), found on remote islands in the southern Indian Ocean. Both are all-white birds that run like a chicken and fly like a pigeon. The pale-faced version is the only one I have photographed. The scientific name for this homely antarctic bird, which early sealers called the sore-eyed pigeon, means snow-white. The bird's eating habits, like its looks, in no way match the image of the legendary princess. Around elephant seal colonies, sheathbills peck over putrid placentas, scavenge carcasses of stillborn pups, pilfer oozing milk from nursing cows, pick at crusty scabs on the necks of wounded bulls

These pale-faced sheathbills are courting. Their nesting season is synchronized to coincide with the feeding of penguin chicks in the nearby gentoo colony.

A pale-faced sheathbill ignores the menacing lunge of a nesting chinstrap penguin. In an hour of scavenging throughout the colony, the sheathbill found nothing more nutritious than penguin droppings.

and beak through every tantalizing turd they find. My friend Bill Munk jokes that "the sheathbill seems to have a smile on its face — a shit-eating smile."

Sheathbills have the same kind of relationship with penguins as they do with elephant seals. The birds hammer unguarded or abandoned penguin eggs, sneak gooey globs of spilled fish and krill and squabble over fresh feces. Dr. Bernard Stonehouse counted 40 sheathbills living around a king penguin colony that he studied on South Georgia. In breeding groups of kings, Adélies and most of the crested penguins, the birds nest too close to one another for sheathbills to wander safely among them without being viciously attacked, so they confine their scavenging to the edges of these colonies. On the other hand, in gentoo and chinstrap colonies, where the nesting birds are spaced farther apart, the bold sheathbills can quietly skulk through the sitting birds, ducking jabs, attacking unattended eggs and scrounging scraps wherever they can find them. The life of the sheathbill may not be as glamorous as that of a penguin, but I marvel at any bird which can make a living from such seemingly unappealing dietary fare.

Skuas (*Catharacta* spp) are egg thieves in a league of their own. Called "seabirds of prey," they resemble gulls and are related to them yet have traits more typical of predatory birds such as hawks and falcons. Their beaks are sharp-edged and hooked, they have curved claws on their webbed feet, their legs are covered with tough, protective scales, and in common with birds of prey, the females are larger and more powerful than their mates. Robert Cushman Murphy was deeply impressed by the skuas he saw in South Georgia, and he wrote about them with admiration: "The skuas look and act like miniature eagles. They fear nothing, never seek to avoid being conspicuous, and by every token of their behavior, they are Lords of the Far South."

Three different species of these rapacious seabirds live where there are penguins. At sea, and for most of the year, skuas scavenge and prey mainly on fish, but when they come ashore to nest, they often select territories adjacent to penguin colonies and supplement their diets by preying on penguin eggs and chicks. For five years, Dr. Euan Young studied the interactions between several hundred territorial pairs of south polar skuas (*Catharacta maccormicki*) and a large colony of Adélie penguins at Cape Bird in Antarctica's Ross Sea. The smallest skua territory had 14 penguin nests, and the largest 1,715. Fiercely territorial, a breeding skua pair aggressively defends its nesting grounds and the penguins within it against all rivals. Should a trespassing skua invade an occupied territory, it may be viciously attacked. Bones can be broken in midair collisions, or the birds can be seriously injured when they grapple and plunge to the ground. If one of the combatants, usually the territorial owner, gets an opening, it may kill the imprudent rival.

Skuas defend the penguins in their territories. They do this not to promote the well-being of the penguins but to monopolize a source of food for themselves, and they watch and check their flightless flock constantly. When penguins fight, the squabble may spill over several adjacent territories and involve 10 adults or more. The opportunistic skuas watch for such rows and routinely fly over to check whether any eggs or chicks are displaced during the commotion. At other times, the skuas regularly tack back and forth over the penguins, flying at an average height of just 6½ to 13 feet (2–4 m). If a skua spots an unguarded egg, it plummets like a rock, snatches the booty and is airborne again in an instant. An exceptionally large gape allows the skua to fly off with an intact penguin egg in its mouth. The success of such overflights often depends upon the element of surprise, but skuas employ even more daring tactics than these.

Researcher Young described three strategies used by south polar skuas against Adélies. In a "jump attack," the skua, with wings raised, rushes and leaps at a standing penguin, striking it high on the body with its outstretched feet and knocking the bird off balance. In an even bolder maneuver, a flying skua glides into a penguin in a "crash flight." The force of the collision may knock the startled penguin into its irate neighbors, which compounds the commotion. Although both the jump attack and the crash flight are successful roughly one-third of the time, they expose the skua to the high risk of injury, so neither method is used very often. A more common ploy is for a skua to tug on a penguin's tail feathers. When the bird swivels to respond, it exposes its eggs to attack. This tactic works even better when two skuas team up. While one bird harries the penguin, the other grabs the eggs. If a skua catches a penguin snoozing on its eggs, it can sometimes jerk its tail feathers so strongly that the sleeping bird is pulled off the nest. Before the penguin can react, the skua scrambles over it and grabs an egg.

Not all the penguins in a colony are equally vulnerable to skua attacks. Those in the center are much better protected. Central nests are often built closer together than those on the periphery, and every nest owner is surrounded by belligerent neighbors with a shared enmity for skuas. It's the nests on the edges of a colony

A predatory skua eats the contents of an infertile gentoo egg that had rolled to the edge of the penguins' nest and was poorly guarded.

that most often come under attack. These birds do not have a protective neighbor on every flank, so it is easier for skuas to get close to them. The situation is even worse for a penguin whose nest is separated enough from the colony's edge to allow skuas to attack from any angle. The eggs in these nests are often doomed.

In most areas where penguins live, there are no land predators, and the nesting adults have nothing to fear. At least, that's what I thought until early 1995. That spring, *Discover* — a highly respected publication — reported in its Breakthroughs in Science, Technology and Medicine department the description of an amazing mammal new to science. Researcher Aprile Pazzo had been studying emperor penguins in a remote corner of Antarctica along the coast of the Ross Sea. One day, the penguins suddenly began to stampede. When Pazzo walked closer to see what had happened, she found one of the penguins sinking into the ice as if into quicksand. The magazine reported: "Somehow, the ice beneath the bird had

A dolphin gull flies over a colony of gentoo penguins in search of displaced eggs and spilled fish. Much smaller than the penguins, the gull must stay clear of the gentoos' powerful beaks.

melted; the penguin was waist-deep in slush. Pazzo tried to help the struggling penguin. She grabbed its wings and pulled. With a heave, she freed the bird. But the penguin wasn't the only thing she hauled from the slush. About a dozen small, hairless, pink molelike creatures had clamped their jaws onto the penguin's lower body. Pazzo managed to capture one of the creatures—the others quickly released their grip and vanished into the slush."

Pazzo described the small mammal as "repulsive" and named it the hot-headed naked ice borer. Apparently, this amazing animal has a rich vascular area on the top of its head that radiates enough heat to allow it to melt tunnels through the ice and hunt penguins, its favorite prey. The magazine continued: "A pack of ice borers will cluster under a penguin and melt the ice and snow it's standing on. When the hapless bird sinks into the slush, the ice borers attack, dispatching it with bites of their sharp incisors. They then carve it up and carry its flesh back to their burrows, leaving behind only webbed feet, a beak and some feathers."

I telephoned distinguished editor Michael Abrams to express my excitement about this new wildlife discovery and how timely it was, considering that I was researching a book about the lives of penguins. He told me the story had prompted more mail than any other in recent memory. You can imagine my shock when he finally confessed that the story was just an April Fools' joke. Suckered by scientists! Is nothing sacred?

Get Cracking

The heavy eggshell of penguins prevents it from cracking prematurely, but there comes a time, of course, when it is crucial that the egg should crack. As in most birds, the hatching penguin chick is completely on its own when it comes to the task of breaking out. It must squirm, kick, stretch and crack itself free. The chick gets no help from its parents. Every hatchling penguin is equipped with an egg tooth—a hard, sharp projection on the tip of its beak that it uses to chisel the inside of the shell until it finally begins to crack.

One year, I monitored the hatching progress of a gentoo chick at a colony in the Falkland Islands. At 8 a.m. on the first day, the egg was starred, a term used to describe a small area of the shell that is finely cracked and raised like a blemish. By early evening of the same day, the chick had chipped a hole through the shell and the tip of its beak was sticking out. The young bird was peeping faintly. By noon the following day, the hatchling had broken free, its down was dry, and it was securely buried under the hot plate of its parent's brood patch. From the time an egg is starred, it usually takes one to three days for a penguin chick to hatch, somewhat longer than most bird species and likely a reflection of the greater thickness of the penguin eggshell.

Dr. Bernard Stonehouse watched many king penguins hatch on South Georgia, observing that "the chick may be heard shortly after the first starring appears on the shell. No assistance is offered by the incubating parents, although considerable interest is shown. Boluses of food are frequently deposited on the hatching shell. A small number of chicks die while hatching, usually because the membranes dry and harden before the emerging chick manages to struggle free. A few which hatched on sites where the parent was standing in running water were drowned as soon as their heads were liberated from the shells."

Inside the egg, the chick is curled with its head tucked tightly against its chest. I've always marveled at how young birds manage

The hatching of the first chick in a clutch of rockhopper eggs often results in the parents' ignoring the second egg. The discarded egg is usually the smaller one.

to free themselves in this cramped position. They succeed with the help of a specialized enlarged muscle on the rear of their necks. Known as the hatching muscle, it allows the chick to straighten its neck and wield the egg tooth with greater force. The muscle atrophies soon after hatching.

Newly hatched penguin chicks are covered with a fine down, the color of which varies among the different species, ranging from silver-gray to dark brown or black. In all chicks, however, the color and pattern differs considerably from that of the adult. The distinctive chick plumage immediately signals the immaturity of the bird, and as a consequence, other adults do not perceive the chicks as rivals. The plumage may in fact elicit parental behavior instead of the aggression typically shown to neighbors. Even so, the system sometimes breaks down. At a rockhopper colony, I watched the murder of a young hatchling by a neighboring adult male.

"When I first spotted the black downy chick," I wrote in my field notes, "it was wobbling between two nests. On one of the nests,

an adult male was brooding a chick of his own, and his mate was standing beside him. Both adults stretched over and screamed a loud threat at the tiny chick, and then the big-beaked male attacked. He shook the chick vigorously and gave it six or seven hard pecks on the body and head, killing it very quickly. The aggressive male continued to peck at the chick periodically for 10 minutes after it was dead."

Among the 15 species that lay two eggs, one egg hatches significantly sooner than the other in all but the yellow-eyed penguin. The hatching interval varies between one and four days but can be as long as seven days in some of the crested penguins. In all of them, the first chick to hatch is the first to be fed, and even within a day, it is larger and stronger than its nestmate. The asynchronous hatching establishes a feeding hierarchy. The latecomer begs less enthusiastically and so is fed less. As a result, its growth is retarded. It may get fed only after its larger sibling is full. In other birds, siblings may actually attack and kill their nestmates, pecking them to

Even when the second egg in a rockhopper nest hatches, it is exceptionally rare for the small chick to survive. It usually starves to death within two weeks.

death or pushing them out of the nest. Between penguin chicks, the competition is nonaggressive – the stronger chick simply monopolizes the feeding, shoving the smaller chick out of the way.

The interval between the hatching of two penguin chicks is a method of "brood reduction," a way for the parent birds to raise at least one strong chick if food is in short supply. In many areas where penguins breed, the year-to-year availability of food is unpredictable, and through brood reduction, birds can match the number of chicks they raise with the prevailing ocean conditions. When food is plentiful, they can raise two chicks. Among the two-egg species, only the crested penguins practice obligatory brood reduction. This means that no matter how plentiful food may be, one chick, usually the one from the smaller egg, either fails to hatch or starves to death within 7 to 10 days of hatching. On several occasions, I've watched rockhopper parents brood one chick and totally ignore their second egg, letting it chill in the cold wind even though the unhatched chick was cheeping through a hole in the shell.

The parent that is on duty at the time the penguin chick hatches may have no food to regurgitate to feed it. Closer to the time of hatching, most penguin parents take short incubation shifts and relieve each other more frequently than they did in the beginning. This ensures that a full-bellied adult will generally show up at the nest within a day or two of the chick's arrival. Even so, most chicks can survive for two to three days without feeding, and in Adélies, that can stretch to seven or eight. They survive by absorbing the remnants of the yolk sac. The yolk in a penguin's egg is relatively large and may have evolved as a necessary trait for the survival of hatchlings whose parents often forage far from the nest and may not return on schedule. Emperor penguins have solved the problem of early chick feeding in the most ingenious way. The female emperor returns in late winter to her mate and her egg after an absence of two months or more. Naturally, her timing may not be precise – the chick may hatch before she arrives. To make matters worse, the attending male parent has generally fasted for more than three months and lost 40 percent of his body weight. He would seem to be in no nutritional state to provide food for a hungry chick. Nonetheless, the improbable happens. Unique among penguins, the adult male emperor secretes a kind of curd from the lining of his esophagus, which he then regurgitates into the imploring beak of his peeping chick.

In composition, the secretion resembles the rich milk of marine mammals such as seals and whales and contains 29 percent fat

The head of a young gentoo chick disappears inside the throat of its parent as it reaches for a meal. This style of feeding lessens the risk of food spillage and loss to scavengers.

The white spur at the tip of the beak of a newly hatched gentoo is an "egg tooth" that the young penguin uses to chip its way out of the egg.

and 59 percent protein. Compare this with the watery nutrition of cow's milk, which contains just 4 percent fat and 3 percent protein. A male emperor may offer his chick multiple meals of this "crop milk," totaling 8 to 10 ounces (226–283 g), allowing the young bird to survive for up to two weeks after hatching, generally enough time for the overdue female to show up.

The temperament of Antarctica, however, can be merciless. One winter, more than 90 percent of the newly hatched emperor chicks at Pointe Géologie starved to death when an unusually wide stretch of unbroken sea ice, more than 300 miles (500 km) in extent, separated the colony from the open sea and prevented the females from returning in time to feed their chicks. Regardless of the reason a female emperor fails to come back on schedule, her mate will never loiter long enough to risk his own survival. In over 35 years, no researcher has ever found a male emperor that fasted himself to death. When the bird reaches a critical minimum weight, somewhere around 53 pounds (24 kg), he jettisons the hapless chick and makes a beeline for the sea.

Chicks Under Foot and Flipper

When a penguin chick hatches, its eyelids are sealed together and remain that way for three or four days. Like so many young nestlings at this age, the chick is an undersized wobbly-necked bag of down that peeps incessantly, "Feed me, feed me, feed me." For the first four weeks of a penguin chick's life and for several weeks afterward, it is guarded constantly by one of its parents. In little penguins, the guarding phase lasts 15 days; in the medium-sized species, three to four weeks; in kings and yellow-eyes, it increases to six or seven weeks; and in emperors, it lasts eight weeks. In most cases, the parents share these duties. The exception is in the crested penguins, where the male does it all, nest-bound for the entire month while the female brings home food for the youngster. The strongly aggressive nature and larger beak and body size of the male crested penguin make it a better bodyguard than the female, and that may be the reason it is the primary guardian of the chick.

Penguin chicks grow quite rapidly. In Adélies, for example, a newly hatched chick weighs just 3 ounces (85 g). It quadruples its weight by day 5, and by day 8, it weighs 25 ounces (710 g). By day 12, the little potbellied tubby weighs 43 ounces (1,220 g) — a fourteenfold increase in less than two weeks.

When you are standing near a penguin nest, it's possible to estimate the rough age of the chick by how a parent guards it. In the first week of a chick's life, the protective adult completely covers the nestling with its body. By the second week, the young penguin has grown enough that its parent simply crouches over it while the chick, swaddled in the adult's feathered belly fold, gawks at the world. By the third week, the chick has grown too big to be brooded easily, and the bottom-heavy youngster squats beside its parent like a miniature Buddha. If it becomes alarmed, it still tries to hide under the adult, but because of its size, it can only bury its head in the brood pouch with its butt left out in the cold. It's a little bit like hiding your head in an oven. By the fourth week, the growing chick begins to explore the area around its nest, but if it gets into trouble or bothers the neighbors, it still has a parent nearby to defend it.

There are a number of reasons penguin chicks need to be guarded so closely in the early weeks of their lives. Other adults, especially failed breeders, may harass the young birds, and in emperor penguins, the harassment can be deadly. Six or seven adults may pounce on a stray chick and trample or maul it to death in the struggle. Determined kidnapper penguins may even take a chick from the feet of its parent, only to abandon it a few hours later. These strong-arm tactics can have a tremendous impact on the chicks of a colony. One season at Cape Washington, in

Two week-old gentoo chicks bury their heads beneath the warmth of their parent's brood patch. The young birds display the same behavior when they are frightened.

above: When food is plentiful, large gentoo chicks may not squabble with each other when a parent returns to the nest to feed them.

right: An adult southern giant petrel "mantles" aggressively beside the carcass of an antarctic fur seal. Its hooked butcher beak is a formidable weapon.

the Ross Sea, more than 80 percent of the chicks in the emperor colony were killed over the course of a month by unsuccessful breeders fighting for possession of them. The parental instinct is so strong in emperors that an adult will carry a frozen and lifeless chick around on its feet, hopelessly trying to nurture it, until the down is completely worn off the tiny bird's body. Biologists believe that emperor chicks are so vulnerable to other adults because the birds do not defend nesting territories. That and their habit of huddling together for warmth allow adults to approach each other freely.

Inclement weather poses another threat to young penguin chicks. It takes about two to three weeks for the down of most chicks to thicken enough so that they can maintain their own body temperature. Until that time, they must be shielded and warmed by their parents. Even in the shelter of a hot-blooded adult, however, the weather can still be a killer. In late 1995, an icy rain pelted a rockhopper colony on the Sea Lion Islands in the Falklands. When I visited the penguins on January 4, five days after the storm, nearly half of the chicks were dead. Island resident David Gray told me that the young birds had been too big for the parents to brood and had gotten soaked and probably perished from hypothermia. Writing about how such storms can affect emperors, French researcher Dr. Pierre Jouventin observed: "Following a severe tempest, it is quite usual to find a hundred or so bodies of chicks buried in tombs of ice formed from particles which were carried by the blizzard. Death from freezing is most likely to occur in chicks weakened by undernourishment....Highest mortality among chicks occurs in September, when the chicks leave the parental incubating pouch but have not yet formed the habit of huddling behind groups of adults for shelter."

A fat, defenseless chick is an irresistible temptation for any predator, and adult penguins must also guard their young against a squad of hungry beaks. In South America and southern Africa, kelp gulls (*Larus dominicanus*) boldly pluck young magellanics, Humboldts and Africans from their nesting burrows; in the Falkland Islands, rapacious striated caracaras (*Phalcoboenus australis*) swoop out of the sky and take gentoo and rockhopper chicks; in the Galápagos Islands, the endemic Galápagos hawk (*Buteo galapagoensis*) and the barn owl (*Tyto alba*) talon any penguin chick that carelessly wanders beyond the safety of its nesting crevice; and all across the sub-Antarctic, butcher-beaked giant petrels (*Macronectes giganteus* and *M. halli*) nab king penguin chicks. Outshadowing the

A gentoo chick, healthy and rippling with fat, dozes in the sun after being fed by its parent.

A male brown skua calls to its larger mate sitting on their two eggs. The pair was nesting less than 200 yards (180 m) from a gentoo penguin colony, which they routinely raided for eggs and chicks.

right: An adult rockhopper begins to vocalize as it approaches its old nest. On hearing its parent's voice, the chick returns to the nest to be fed.

reputation of all these winged predators are, once again, those legendary seabirds of prey, the predatory skuas.

In the Falklands, I watched a large female brown skua (*Catharacta antarctica*) muscle against the wind above a colony of rockhoppers huddling over their chicks. One moment, the skua was aloft above a phalanx of threatening beaks, and the next, she had dropped from sight amid a blur of flippers and golden crests. When she reappeared, she had a small chick in her beak. The skua swallowed the live bundle of down in a single gulp, never missing a wing beat.

Death may come more slowly for larger penguin chicks. After a skua has dragged or carried a chick away from the protection of its parents, the messy business begins. Skuas lack an effective killing beak, so they dispatch their prey with repeated blows to the head and neck. Penguin skin is very tough and difficult to tear, so a skua will often attack a chick around its cloaca, where the tissue is more easily penetrated, then proceed to disembowel the victim. Such attacks may be quite drawn out and gruesome. I watched a pair of skuas kill a young gentoo chick in this way, and it took all the

Streaks of guano radiate outward from the nests in a gentoo colony in the Falkland Islands. Both the adults and the chicks contribute to the sunburst design.

scientific objectivity I could muster not to interfere and either rescue the chick or end its misery quickly.

The size of chick that a skua can handle depends on how strongly the wind is blowing. To pluck one from the center of a cluster of penguins, the skua must be able to drop and lift off quickly. Biologist Dr. Euan Young calculated that in calm winds, a determined skua could lift 16 ounces (450 g) and could drag and bounce 21 ounces (600 g). In a stronger wind, say, 15 miles per hour (24 km/h), its lift limit increased by another 3½ ounces (100 g). On the ground, the powerful skua could drag its own body weight, up to 3½ pounds (1.5 kg).

Skuas don't always have it their way; sometimes, penguins get a chance to mete out their own punishment. Young believes that it is not uncommon for a skua to be caught by a penguin. When he observed a colony of Adélies over a 44-hour period, the feisty penguins nabbed south polar skuas on at least nine occasions. Young thought that the flailing flipper of a penguin could break the wing of a skua and that this posed the greatest risk to skuas. In his authoritative book *Skua and Penguin: Predator and Prey,* Young recounted the thrashing of an inexperienced skua that got caught trying to retrieve a dead penguin chick from the center of a colony: "It was held and attacked by up to 10 penguins at a time as it fought its way across seven meters [23 ft] and through 11 nests to reach the margin 51 seconds after first being caught. It could neither fly nor stand after reaching the relative safety of open ground outside the margin." The wounded skua had been trespassing in the territory of another pair. Young then intervened to save it from being killed by the resident birds.

Though skuas get their share of lickings, that fact never seemed to soften the attitude of early polar travelers toward these seabirds, which historically were often maligned and mistreated. The authors of a report from Byrd's Second Antarctic Expedition of 1933-35 bluntly opined: "The drama of antarctic bird life is not without its villain. Theft and pillage, murder, cannibalism and infanticide, these crimes are all in the repertory of the South Polar Skua."

Others employed harsher weapons than rhetoric. The French Antarctic Expedition of 1948-53 used bombs to rid its camp of skuas. Some early travelers with a sadistic streak would discard burning cigarette butts near loafing skuas to watch them squabble over and gulp down the unfamiliar objects. Another trick was to lace wads of meat with hot chili powder and chuckle as the unsuspecting birds swallowed the food and then regurgitated it almost immediately because of irritation to their stomachs. Sometimes, one skua after another would swallow and regurgitate the same piece of treated meat until one of them finally kept it down. The more birds that gulped it down, the funnier the visitors seemed to find it.

Penguin parents don't spend all their time scanning the skies and fending off skuas and other predators; after all, they have a family to feed, and these chicks have appetites that are hard to satiate. While one parent guards the youngsters, the other forages at sea. The distance a parent must travel from the colony to find food generally determines how frequently a chick is fed. Commonly, the interval between meals in kings and emperors may be three days or longer. Adélie, chinstrap, royal, macaroni, rockhopper and magellanic chicks are fed more often than that—typically, every one to three days. The chicks of all the other species of penguins usually receive a meal every day or so.

Naturally, the meal size increases with the age of the chick. In chinstraps, for example, chicks less than 10 days old gulp down meals averaging 6½ ounces (185 g), about the weight of the filet mignon served in many fine restaurants. From age 20 to 40 days, the young chinstraps consume an average of 18½ ounces (527 g) per meal, but some may gobble down monster meals weighing more than 1½ pounds (680 g)! After such a meal, they must truly be too stuffed to squawk.

The chicks of most species of birds have evolved some way to stimulate their parents to feed them. In songbirds, it may be a colorful pattern that is visible when the young birds gape. This not only attracts the attention of the adults but serves as a target for them. In other species, such as gulls, the chicks must peck a specific colored spot or band on the parent's beak, called a releaser point, which then prompts the parent to regurgitate food. A penguin chick simply vibrates its beak against that of its parent, and when the adult bird gapes, the chick wedges its bill inside and gobbles up the slimy regurgitant directly.

In medical school, I learned about the gastrocolic reflex. When food goes in the front end of our bodies, our large intestine promptly makes room by moving things along and out the rear exit. If you watch penguin chicks being fed, you soon realize that humans are not the only creatures with this convenient intestinal reflex. I recorded this indelicate aspect of penguin biology a number of times in my field notes: "Shortly after they are fed, young rockhopper chicks bend forward and eject feces with an explosive squirt. The gooey guano sometimes hits a sleeping neighbor in the face. The sprayed bird simply shakes its head a few times, and the whitewash slowly drips off the tip of its beak, after which it falls back to sleep. When a gentoo defecates, it perches on the edge of its nest and lets the fluid fly. Every nest has a ring of white streaks radiating out from it like the spokes of a wheel."

Having worked on a farm with chickens as a boy and shoveled the stinking stuff until my back was stiff, I consider myself somewhat of a guano aficionado. Although I've never taken a shovel to a penguin colony, I have studied this aspect of their lives, possibly with more interest than is healthy. A keen naturalist can generally tell what a penguin has been eating by the color of its droppings. When a penguin eats squid, the ink in the animal reacts with the acid in the bird's stomach to produce yellow guano. When it eats fish, its droppings are whitish gray, and a diet of krill tints the turds pink. For a while, I was stumped by green guano. Author

Rockhopper chicks of various ages cluster together in a protective crèche. This phase of a chick's life lasts for several weeks.

Murray Levick, who wrote one of the early books on penguins, knew exactly what it meant: "During fasting, the excreta of Adélies are green and bile-stained and are squirted clear of [the nests] for a distance of a foot or more so that each nest has the appearance of a flower with bright green petals radiating from its center."

Levick noted that the chicks also contribute to the artistry of the family nest, "because they lie with their heads under the old birds' bellies and their hindquarters just presenting themselves so that they may add their own little decorative offerings, petal by petal."

More Chick Chatter

Penguin biologists call the second and longest stage of chick rearing the "post-guarding phase." The young penguins have grown large enough to be left temporarily on their own, and both parents are now free to go to sea at the same time. In this way, the adults can deliver more meals to the chicks, whose appetites have kept pace with their growth. The behavior of the unguarded chicks differs among the various species of penguins. In the burrow- and crevice-nesting banded penguins and the little penguin, the chicks tend to be loners, loitering by themselves at the mouth of their nest chambers. In some cases, they may form small bands of five or six neighboring chicks. Yellow-eyed penguins most often nest far apart and in dense vegetation. As a result, the chicks of these birds also stay alone or with a single nestmate. The chicks of the other penguin species, such as those of kings, emperors and the crested and brush-tailed penguins, herd together in sizable groups called crèches. Common among a variety of birds, crèches are seen in flamingos, ostriches, rheas, emus and eider ducks, all of which have lifestyles quite different from those of penguins.

Penguin crèches vary in size. Those of Snares penguins contain up to 30 downy chicks, Adélies can have over 100 in a group, and king chicks commonly gather in clusters of 20 to 30 young birds, although in the winter season, kings may form immense crèches of 1,000 or more chicks. In rockhopper penguins, not only does the size of the crèche vary but its composition and location within the colony change slightly from day to day. It's likely that the same applies to most of the other species as well. Rockhopper chicks tend to cluster in spaces within the colony where there are no nests. In this way, the young birds avoid the menacing beaks of adults still

guarding their chicks. All the better if the unoccupied areas are in the center of a colony, where the chicks are surrounded by adults and shielded somewhat from the preying eyes of skuas.

Initially, a crèche contains just two or three chicks, but it can grow larger very quickly. Dr. Euan Young documented the transition in Adélie penguins in the Ross Sea. The first chicks were left unguarded on December 30. By January 3, 16 percent of them were alone, and two days later, that number had increased to 30 percent. By January 10, all but 1 percent of the chicks had joined crèches. In the crested penguins, the crèching phase may begin with neighboring chicks simply standing together at a nest guarded by one of the male parents. In the Falklands, I photographed a male adult rockhopper guarding three large downy chicks. In the past, this behavior led to the false belief that crested penguins sometimes raised two or three chicks. The main reason for Adélie chicks and those of gentoos, chinstraps and the crested penguins to cluster

A crèche of king penguin chicks on South Georgia is surrounded by a throng of adults. Remarkably, every adult can identify the voice of its own offspring among the imploring chirps of hundreds of chicks.

In the 1800s, sealers called king penguin chicks "oakum boys" because their feathers looked exactly like large handfuls of oakum, the rope fibers used to caulk the seams of wooden ships.

together is as a defense against predators, especially skuas. Although a skua could rush into a crèche, scatter the chicks and grab one of them, it rarely does. Certainly the young penguins pose very little threat to an adult skua, and it's a mystery why the predators don't commonly attack the chicks when they are clumped together like this. When a skua approaches a crèche, the youngsters bunch together tighter and sometimes shuffle away as a group. Typically, a skua targets one of the imprudent stragglers on the perimeter of a crèche, so a chick is usually safe if it stays tightly tucked within the group.

The first chicks in a colony to be left unguarded are at the greatest risk from skuas. The young unfortunates may get caught between predatory skuas and pugnacious adult penguins. Young witnessed several instances where an Adélie chick was dragged away by a skua, escaped and ran back among some nesting penguins only to be driven out to the edge of the colony by the belligerent adults. There, the same skuas were waiting to attack the chick again. Another reason penguin chicks crowd into a crèche is for protection against the weather. Just as adult emperors huddle together during the winter, a young penguin chick loses less body heat when it is crammed into a crèche than it would if it were out in the open on its own. King and emperor chicks are generally too large for skuas to take, and the chicks of these species form crèches primarily for this reason alone.

In 1960, most penguin biologists believed that chicks were coaxed or actually driven into crèches by their parents and that afterward, a few of the adult birds stayed behind to guard the group and protect the young penguins from predators. They also believed that once a chick became a member of a crèche, it severed all attachments with its parents and that the adults fed the chicks communally, disregarding family relationships. The truth is far more interesting.

To begin with, it seems that chicks wander away from the nest and gang together of their own volition. The parents do not drive them away. In one case, I saw a rockhopper chick leave its male parent alone on the nest, waddle over and wedge itself into a crèche. The male did nothing to induce it to leave, nor did he try to herd the chick back. In some cases, however, when food is scarce and it is difficult for the parents to feed their chicks, they may leave them unguarded earlier than usual, before the young birds have the natural urge to wander and group together. These small, undernourished chicks are easy prey for skuas and often do not survive.

About the time that chicks start to gather in crèches, many penguin colonies are invaded by nonbreeding adults along with other adults that tried to breed earlier but failed and have returned to reclaim their deserted territories. These newly arrived adults are the birds early observers mistakenly thought were the "nurses" and "guardians" of the chicks. Mostly, they wander around and cause havoc in a colony, harassing and pecking the chicks and challenging the breeding adults that are shuffling back and forth between the sea and the colony busily feeding their offspring. Nevertheless, the wanderers may indirectly benefit a penguin colony. These irascible adult birds readily chase any skua that lands near a colony. Gangs of them may even flush a skua from its nest and, in the attack, inadvertently crush the bird's eggs or leave them open to predation by another skua.

Another misconception about penguins was that an adult bird would feed any hungry chick which begged, whether the young penguin was related to it or not. Altruism is a wonderful concept that can ensure the survival of a group, but for the individual, it is an evolutionary dead end. No creature on Earth today is a full-time altruist. Virtually everyone and everything is driven primarily by the selfish imperative to perpetuate its own genes. This is the basic tenet of current evolutionary theory, and penguins are no exception. For this reason, a penguin parent rarely, if ever, feeds any chick but its own.

After roiling in the surf, clambering up cliff and slope and crossing sea ice and hummock, penguin parents returning from a fishing trip usually hustle back to their old nest site. As they get close, they trumpet and scream their arrival. Young chicks recognize the sound of their parents' voices. As soon as they hear the adults, they immediately leave the crèche and return to their old nest to be fed. One researcher used tape recordings of adult calls to dupe Adélie chicks and lure them out of the crèche. In 90 percent of the trials, the correct chick—and only that chick—left the security of the crèche and waddled over to its old nest. Crèchemates are not always so well-behaved, and a parent's call to dinner may be answered by chicks other than its own. When this happens, usually all it takes is a few sound pecks or a couple of hard whacks with a flipper to dissuade even the most insistent of outsiders.

Just as penguin chicks know their parents by voice, a parent knows the distinctive chirps of its own chicks. When an Adélie chick hatches, its chirp is quite variable and sounds much like the other chicks around it. In fact, if one newly hatched chick is swapped for another, the foster parents will readily accept the chicks. However, by the time a young Adélie is 3 weeks of age, its voice has become distinctive so that it is individually recognizable—a crucial development for parental acceptance once the young bird is left alone. At this stage, even if a chick is painted to disguise its identity, the moment it starts to peep, a parent will accept and feed it no matter how unfamiliar the young bird may look.

When two chicks survive to the crèching age, mealtimes can get crowded. One way for a parent to lessen the confusion is to take the chicks out for a jog. These so-called feeding chases are common in the brush-tailed penguins—gentoos, Adélies and chinstraps. While in the Falklands, I entered the following observation in my journal:

"It's rush hour in the gentoo colony, and there is a steady stream of adults, in threes and fours, hurrying across the sand flats, weaving past clumps of yellow-flowered beach cabbage. As the birds near the colony, their waddle slows, and by the time they reach it, they look like commuters returning after a weary day, their heads sagging with fatigue. At the edge, each bird stops and seems to survey the throng as if deciding what it should do next. Sometimes, it trumpets, but often, it just wades into the clutter of adults and chicks. Suddenly, the chase is on, and the adult bird appears to be running for its life, closely followed by two imploring chicks. The eagerness of the chicks can be so great that they run into the rear of the adult and step on its tail. I sometimes wonder whether the chicks might not keep running right up their parent's back if the adult stopped without warning.

"The dogged chicks shadow the parent's every dodge and turn and are remarkably fast despite their potbellied profiles. As they run along, they chirp loudly and flap their flippers limply. A chase often lasts a minute or two, passing through the colony in a zigzag course, along one edge and then back through the crowd again. Invariably, one of the chicks tires and drops out of the race. Shortly after that, the adult stops and allows the remaining runner

to catch up if it has lagged behind. Often, the first thing the adult does is give the chick a firm peck on the head or back, possibly to keep it in line, but the youngster is not deterred, and it continues to chirp and beg. Soon a slimy wad of regurgitated fish slides down the parent's beak into the gape of the chick—the reward for perseverance."

I remember watching documentaries on television 25 years ago in which the narrator described feeding chases as a way for parents to exercise their chubby chicks. Apparently, it also helped adults to recognize which chicks were theirs, the assumption being that the most tenacious chicks were those pursuing their own parents and the chase for chow was a convenient way to separate outsiders. Today, scientists believe there are other reasons for a penguin parent to lead its chicks on a chase. In his classic book *The Penguins,* researcher Dr. Tony Williams argues that a feeding chase saps energy from a chick, leads it away from the protection of its crèche, leaving it more vulnerable to skua predation, and possibly disorients the young bird. Clearly, such risks must be balanced with a strong benefit, and that benefit is increased efficiency of feeding. A meal

A king penguin chick will beg food from any adult standing nearby. If the adult is not its parent, the chick may be pecked or slapped with a stiff flipper for its efforts.

It is easy to see why young emperor penguin chicks are chosen as models for children's stuffed toys, and are the stars of cartoons and animated movies.

spilled is a meal wasted, since neither an adult penguin nor a chick will retrieve food once it drops on the ground, no matter how simple a task that may seem. Jostling chicks spill meals, and the easiest way for a parent to prevent this waste is to run the chicks and separate them so that they can't interfere with each other.

Spilled krill is not a waste for everyone. Waste not, want not is one of my mother's favorite sayings and perfectly describes the life of the sheathbill. During the penguin chick-rearing season, spilled krill and fish from feeding frenzies are a vital part of the sheathbill's diet—so much so that these scavengers nest almost exclusively in association with penguin colonies and provision their chicks on a steady diet of meals pilfered from penguins. The furtive way they do their dirty work is part of the reason I found these birds so interesting to watch. On the Falklands, I noted how experience pays off: "Sheathbills seem well aware of the dangerously sharp bill of a penguin. When one spots some spilled krill beside a nest, it approaches carefully with a watchful eye on the beaks looming over it. In one instance, a sheathbill made three or four rushes in an attempt to grab a morsel, but the penguin near it kept lunging at the scavenger, and it failed to reach its prize. A bolder sheathbill drove the first bird away, then snuck around behind the penguin, out of its field of vision, and nabbed the krill on its first attempt."

Krill and fish spilled by chance are not plentiful enough to satisfy the appetite of the sheathbill. To shift the odds in its favor, the resourceful scavenger directly interferes with penguins feeding their chicks. This strategy is especially effective at the end of feeding chases, when the penguin parents have conveniently led their chicks away from other neighboring penguins that might spoil the sheathbill's game plan. The sheathbill's modus operandi is simple: Watch for hungry chicks chasing their parents and then get close to them. Adult penguins commonly regurgitate 6 to 12 globs of food per feeding session, so the sheathbill can afford to wait for just the right moment to strike. That happens when the adult has the chick's beak in its mouth. At that instant, the sheathbill flies at the head of the chick, sometimes pecking it. The startled youngster usually ducks and pulls its beak away, but it is too late for the parent to prevent the bolus of food from falling to the ground. In the flap of a flipper, the thief makes off with the gooey goods.

Starving Kings

In most penguins, the post-guarding phase of chick rearing lasts one to three months, a phase that is shortest in the little penguin and longest in the emperor. The common pattern is for the chicks to fledge and scatter at sea early enough in the breeding season that the parents still have time to molt and replace their worn feathers before the onset of winter. It's different for the king penguin, however—very different. For these birds, the post-guarding phase lasts a remarkable 10 to 13 months, three to four times longer than any other penguin and one of the longest in the bird world. Chick rearing starts one summer, carries through the winter and finishes up the following spring or summer.

As it is with any penguin, surviving the rigors of that first winter is one of the greatest challenges faced by king penguin chicks, and the way they do it is a marvel of avian physiology. The staggered breeding cycle of king penguins that I described in Chapter 3 results in chicks facing the hardships of winter at different stages of growth. The fortunate chicks that hatch in January commonly weigh 24 to 26 pounds (11–12 kg) at the start of the season, about 80 percent of their adult weight. Of course, the ones that hatch later are smaller, and the chicks that hatch in April may weigh just 9 to 11 pounds (4–5 kg) when the first storms of winter strike.

Just as the weather deteriorates in winter, so does the young king's food supply. Instead of being fed every three or four days, the chick is now fed every three or four weeks. The parents return independently, delivering up to 6½ pounds (3 kg) of fish and squid a visit, and each makes two or three visits over the winter. These are the starvation rations recorded by Dr. Bernard Stonehouse for king chicks on South Georgia, and this is as good as it gets. On Îles Crozet, home to 500,000 breeding pairs—half of the world's population—the parent birds feed their chicks just once every 39 days, and the young birds get only three meals in the whole winter. Some parents on Îles Crozet do not return even once, forcing their chicks to fast for up to five months. In this case, a 26-pound (12 kg) penguin chick can waste away to a 9-pound (4 kg) sack of feathers and bones—a 68 percent reduction in weight.

Remarkably, chicks can starve to even lighter weights. French researchers found 11 chicks that weighed an average 6½ pounds (3 kg) dying of starvation on Îles Crozet. No other bird fasts this long, and although some mammals, such as hibernating bears and migrating great whales, may fast longer, they lose a smaller percentage of their body weight. The king penguin chick is more resistant to starvation than possibly any other warm-blooded creature on Earth.

With such meager rations, anything a king penguin chick can do to save energy is beneficial. These endearing birds are cloaked in thick brown down that makes them look like fur-coated spectators at a 1920s sporting event. Sealers in the 1800s called the chicks "oakum boys," because they looked exactly like large handfuls of oakum—the loose fibers obtained by picking old rope to pieces—which were used to caulk the seams of wooden ships. Even with their thick feathers, the young penguins commonly group together in crèches to conserve energy. On South Georgia, Stonehouse counted one giant crèche that contained 2,400 chicks! Still, many king penguin chicks die of starvation. The overall chick mortality on Îles Crozet is roughly 50 percent, the greatest losses occurring in September and October, just as the parents are beginning to feed their chicks more frequently again. But for some starvelings, it's too little, too late.

The presence of so many weak and dying penguin chicks is not missed by predators, especially the giant petrels. The winter colonies of king penguin chicks supply a fresh source of food to the petrels in a season of relative scarcity. Not only do these birds

clean up the casualties of the season, but they readily attack and kill any chicks too weak to muster a defense.

For the king penguin chicks that survive the weather, the fasting and the predators, the spring season marks the end of one of the greatest ordeals of their lives. Parents begin feeding them on a regular basis and bring meals every four to six days. As a result, the young penguins rapidly regain their lost weight, and by December, they fledge and finally complete their growth, some 14 to 16 months after they began life inside an egg.

Winter is the most difficult time for king penguin chicks. They may fast for five months and lose 68 percent of their body weight. No other bird fasts as long or loses as much weight.

CHAPTER FIVE

Breakfast, Lunch and Dinner

In Neumayer Channel, along the Antarctic Peninsula, the sea ice disappears for just a few months each summer. The flush of invertebrate life that results is harvested by penguins nesting nearby.

Southern Seafood

Penguins everywhere eat three main foods: fish, squid and crustaceans. Knowing some of the details of how these three groups of marine animals live is the first step in understanding how penguins harvest the sea.

Let's begin with the fish of the Southern Ocean, where the greatest number of penguins occur. When you compare the average depth and area of all the oceans on Earth, the Southern Ocean is possibly the largest marine ecosystem in the world, yet only 120 species of fish live there, a remarkably small number considering that there are roughly 28,000 species of fish worldwide. The reason for this paucity of fish is that the Southern Ocean is a cold, deep ocean with long, dark winters and no shallow-water connection bridging it with any of the other oceans. Because of this isolation, 90 percent of the fish of the Southern Ocean are found nowhere else.

The Southern Ocean's great depth also influences the lack of fish diversity. The average depth of the continental shelf rimming the other oceans is a relatively shallow 425 feet (130 m). The continental shelf surrounding Antarctica is an average 1,300 to 2,000 feet (400–600 m) deep and can plunge to a crushing 3,300 feet (1,000 m). A shallow continental shelf is an important nursery area

left: King penguins may dive more than 1,000 feet (300 m) when hunting. These handsome seabirds specialize in preying on squid and lanternfish.

for the early growth of young fish. In northern polar waters, for example, these shelf areas spawn great schools of Atlantic cod, capelin, herring and sand lance. In contrast, the deep, dark depths of the antarctic continental shelf support no such shoaling fish, and these species are conspicuously absent from the Southern Ocean. Instead, many of the adult fish of the Southern Ocean either hunker near the bottom or patrol the underside of the sea ice, although the juveniles of a number of species do spend some time in open water during their early lives. The unique distribution of fish in the Southern Ocean dictates that penguins be accomplished divers, since they must often search for this finned food on the seafloor, sometimes at incredible depths.

Although the Antarctic and the sub-Antarctic cannot boast large schools of fish, such is not the case in many temperate regions where penguins live, especially in the ocean areas where banded and little penguins are found. The Humboldt and Benguela currents, in particular, support dense schools of anchovies, sardines and pilchards, all of which are preyed upon by the three species of banded penguins that live in these areas. The fish schools, in fact, are so immense that they have been harvested commercially for decades, and this human competition continues to threaten the food supply of the local penguins and the other resident seabirds.

Squid are the second major group of marine animals that penguins find palatable. All squid are carnivores that feed on the same things penguins do — namely, fish, crustaceans and other squid — except squid do it differently.

Predatory squid are the largest invertebrates on Earth, reaching lengths of up to 52½ feet (16 m). These are the same giants which battle sperm whales (*Physeter macrocephalus*) in depths below 3,200 feet (1,000 m) and which attacked the futuristic submarine of the ever courageous Kirk Douglas in the 1954 Hollywood classic *20,000 Leagues Under the Sea*. Squid subdue their prey with a cluster of long, muscular tentacles; typically, they have 10 of them that they can tangle around a victim. Each ropy tentacle has several rows of powerful suckers, many of which may be armed with rings of hooked teeth to improve the animal's deadly grip. Once the prey is grabbed, it is quickly drawn toward the squid's beaklike jaws at the base of the tentacles. There, the hapless victim is summarily decapitated or given a lethal bite.

Presumably, the squid species tackled by penguins are somewhat smaller. The stomach of one magellanic penguin from the coast of Argentina contained 22 squid that weighed a total of nine

The bold black-and-white bands on the sides of the magellanic penguin may startle schools of fish, causing the prey to become disorganized and easier to catch.

On South Georgia, a group of king penguins fords a glacial melt-water stream on its way back to the colony.

pounds (4 kg). The small squid species commonly hunted by little penguins in Australia weigh just slightly more than one-third of an ounce (10 g) each. Scientists think that emperors probably take the largest squid of any penguin, tangling with tentacled prey up to two feet (60 cm) long. My question is, How does a penguin — even one as large as an emperor — manage to swallow a rubber-bodied creature that size whose 10 suckered arms must surely be entwined around the bird's head even as it struggles for dear life?

The seafood most commonly associated with penguins is crustaceans and, in particular, krill. The term krill is not a technical one with a precise meaning, and the name has often been used to describe any kind of invertebrate food eaten by whales; for example, copepods in the Bay of Fundy, mysid shrimp along the western coast of Vancouver Island and lobster krill in the Chilean fjords. Even so, the name krill is generally applied to a small group of crustaceans called euphausiids — shrimp look-alikes — of which there are 11 species in the Southern Ocean. One of the euphausiids,

Euphausia superba, which has no common name, vastly outnumbers all other euphausiids and is the food eaten by more penguins than any other. For example, the millions of chinstraps that breed on the South Sandwich Islands may consume a staggering nine million pounds (4 million kg) of this krill every day.

The feature that makes *Euphausia superba* such an attractive prey to penguins is that it swarms in dense schools, some of which can glut even the most populous penguin colonies. The size and shape of these swarms vary considerably, although the area covered generally ranges between a few square yards and 720 square yards (600 m²), and 98 percent of the swarms contain less than a ton of krill. It's the rare "super-swarms" that capture our attention. These contain truly impressive quantities of krill packed into a single dense school, some of which may be miles in diameter and visible as dense, dark patches of red at the water's surface. The largest super-swarm I've heard of was sighted near Elephant Island, at the tip of the Antarctic Peninsula, on March 7, 1981. The crowd of krill was at least 650 feet (200 m) deep and spread over 60 square miles (155 km²). Some of the samples netted by scientists contained 283 krill per cubic foot (10,000/m³). When the researchers extrapolated these values over the entire swarm, they estimated that it contained as much as 10 million tons (9 billion kg) of krill.

Such super-swarms may remain intact for some time and move considerable distances. One school of krill was tracked for 18 days and traveled over 135 miles (220 km). The challenge for penguins preying on krill is to locate these highly mobile, relatively small, dense patches of prey. As I discussed in Chapter 3, penguins are able to do this in part because they nest in colonies and hunt in groups, where an individual can profit from the chance discoveries of other colony members.

Krill and squid are not without some defense against prowling penguins. Many of them have a daily pattern of migration, as do some fish. At night, under cover of darkness, they swim toward the water's surface, where they forage on plankton and on the plankton-feeders in the upper 300 feet (100 m) of the water column. Then, before daylight breaks, they retreat to the safety of deeper water, between 800 and 1,600 feet (250–500 m), a depth beyond the diving range of most penguins. It's a good strategy, but it fails often enough to feed well over 50 million penguins in the Southern Ocean alone.

Penguins are the most important avian predators in this entire marine ecosystem. Even though roughly 60 species of seabirds

range over the Southern Ocean, penguins comprise up to 98.5 percent of the avian biomass. Another way of saying this is that out of every 35 ounces (1,000 g) of seabird flesh and feathers found in the Southern Ocean, all but a mere 0.05 ounce (1.5 g) is part of a penguin.

Sea Hunting

During the breeding season, a penguin may make dozens of feeding trips to the sea, sometimes to fatten up after a stint of fasting on the nest or to provision its constantly hungry chicks. When scientists first began to study breeding penguins, the birds' life at sea was a great mystery. Shore-bound researchers could only watch and wonder where the birds went when they left each time. How fast did they travel, how far did they go, how often and how deep did they dive, and how much food did they bring back to their chicks? In the past 20 years, improved satellite technology and the miniaturization of instruments has enabled scientists to answer many of these questions, and some of the discoveries are quite surprising.

As I have mentioned, penguins are inveterate groupies and prefer to do almost everything in a bunch; heading out to sea is no exception. On the ice-rimmed shore of Paulet Island, on the Antarctic Peninsula, I witnessed the reaction of an Adélie penguin when the group left without it and made the following entry in my field notes: "Like a black-and-white wave, two dozen birds spilled over the edge of the ice shelf and disappeared into the dark water. One of them at the rear of the group hesitated for a moment, and suddenly, it was left standing alone on the ice. The abandoned bird ran around in circles with its flippers elevated, seemingly agitated by its predicament and torn between its fear of the dangers in the water and the strong urge to stay with its companions. The urge to follow was the stronger, and the penguin leaped off the ice and disappeared."

Penguins can't count, but they certainly seem able to distinguish between a large group of their kind and a small one. Adélie researcher Dr. Dietland Müller-Schwarze believes that parties of penguins departing from the beach observe the size of groups coming in. When groups larger than 25 birds return without mishap, the penguins waiting on shore are more likely to dive in and swim away. Roughly one-third of the groups of this size trigger waiting penguins to leave. In contrast, when five penguins or fewer

Adélie penguins tumble into the water like synchronized swimmers. Traveling as part of a group lessens the individual's risk from underwater predators such as leopard seals, which often lurk along the edges of ice shelves.

return to the beach in a group, their arrival prompts others to leave in just 11 percent of cases. Why is it apparently so important for penguins to depart as a group? The answer, in a word, is predators. Killer whales, leopard seals, fur seals and sea lions patrol the inshore waters near many penguin colonies. Traveling in a group offers the individual penguin a number of benefits that lessen the risk from predators. To begin with, a group of penguins has more eyes to detect a predator's silent liquid approach, so there is less chance of a surprise attack. As well, an individual bird fleeing as a member of a group is less likely to be singled out by a predator. As a final advantage, a group member can sometimes use a traveling companion to shield itself from danger. It's noteworthy that such apparently selfish yet successful behavior is just the kind of behavior most likely to be passed on to future generations and perpetuated within the species. After all, self-sacrificing altruists end up eaten and are therefore unable to pass on any traits to the next generation.

Depending on the size of a colony, penguins may leave the beach in groups of up to 100 birds, but parties of a dozen or two are more common. In the danger zone near shore, where underwater predators are most likely to be lurking, many species of penguins porpoise for the first part of the trip, as this method of travel is more difficult for a predator to track. A large group leaving the shore like this may stay together, seeking safety in numbers, until it is a few miles from the beach. At that point, the penguins commonly separate into smaller foraging groups which often contain no more than a dozen individuals.

A penguin's time at sea is roughly divided into four phases: traveling to the feeding area; searching for food once it has found a likely hunting location; catching the prey after it is sighted; and returning to the colony. When a penguin is safely out to sea, it typically switches from porpoising to "travel diving." Travel dives are short, less than two minutes in duration, and generally shallow, with the bird swimming no deeper than 10 feet (3 m), and they are punctuated by frequent rests at the surface that last for 20 to 30 seconds. Penguins on a feeding trip don't meander; they seem to have a destination in mind and travel in a relatively direct course. What is not known, however, is what clues the birds use to decide when they should start searching for prey. It could be the water temperature, currents, turbidity, depth, topography of the bottom or even wave heights. This aspect of a penguin's life remains a complete mystery.

Interspersed with these adult magellanics are a number of 1-year-old birds. By traveling with experienced adults, young penguins probably learn hunting techniques and avoidance of predators.

The yellow-eyed penguin feeds close to shore and usually spends less than a day or two on its feeding trips.

As you would predict, the distance a penguin will travel from the colony on a feeding trip depends on the stage of its nesting cycle. Over the course of incubation, for example, a bird may be at sea for several weeks at a stretch. The male emperor may stay out for a month regaining the weight it lost during the three months it was onshore. During these protracted stints at sea, a penguin may travel hundreds of miles. Of course, the largest penguins travel the farthest: kings may cover 300 miles (500 km) or more, and big-bodied emperors close to 950 miles (1,500 km). Once the chicks hatch, the feeding trips are shorter and, in the majority of species, last just a few days at most and cover fewer than 36 miles (60 km). Some penguins that feed relatively close to shore, such as gentoos and yellow-eyes, leave and return in less than 12 hours.

Compared with flying seabirds, penguins are much more restricted in the distances they can cover on a feeding trip; there is roughly a tenfold difference in traveling speed. Penguins offset their reduced feeding range with their ability to dive and search waters beyond the reach of other seabirds, and they can dive deeper and stay down longer than any other group of birds. Most species of penguins are able to reach depths up to 300 feet (100 m) and stay submerged for five to six minutes, although they commonly forage in water much shallower than this, 30 to 165 feet (10–50 m) being typical, and stay under for just a minute or two. Once again, the kings and emperors are the record setters. One deep-diving king plunged to 1,060 feet (325 m). This pales in comparison to the feat of an emperor that dove to an amazing 2,110 feet (643 m). Emperors hold the time record for staying underwater as well — an incredible 22 minutes. By comparison, the human record for a breath-held dive was set in 1993 by a Cuban named Francisco "Pipin" Ferreras, who was underwater for two minutes nine seconds and dove to a depth of 410 feet (125 m). The sperm whale is the deepest-diving warm-blooded creature on Earth and has been recorded at depths of 6,562 feet (2,000 m). There is indirect evidence that these squid-hunting toothed whales may even reach depths of almost 9,850 feet (3,000 m) and stay submerged for nearly two hours.

To track a penguin's diving behavior, scientists use an instrument called a time-depth recorder, which they glue to the bird's back. With this instrument, they can easily detect the penguin's transition from the traveling phase to the searching part of a feeding trip. Once a penguin begins to search for prey, its dives become deeper and of a different style, tracing a V- or U-shaped path. In a V-shaped dive, the bird simply dives to a certain depth, then

bounces back to the surface; in a U-shaped dive, the bird swims at the maximum depth for a distance before rising to the surface again. Although the bottom portion of a U-shaped dive may occur in midwater levels, it often coincides with the seafloor.

A penguin will make many dives during a typical feeding trip. In one study of gentoos on the South Shetland Islands, the birds made 192 dives per trip; others on South Georgia averaged 103 dives per outing. One remarkable gentoo made 460 dives in just 15 hours. In other studies, macaronis on South Georgia made up to 677 dives per trip, and chinstraps in the South Orkney Islands sometimes made 257 dives during a trip. Kings, which usually stay at sea longer than any of these species, averaged 601 dives per trip when hunting the waters around South Georgia.

Other than simply bumping into food during the progress of a dive, it's not completely clear how a penguin finds its food. Birds may monitor the feeding success of other penguins in the group,

When the tide went out at this Adélie colony, the shorefast ice dropped by nearly 5 feet (1.5 m) making it extremely hard for penguins to leave or return.

and when one of them finds a school of fish or krill, the others may simply share in the discovery. At times, penguins may home in on the feeding frenzies of other seabirds to locate their meals. Groups of up to 20 Snares penguins have been seen feeding in association with petrels and shy albatrosses in the same way that Galápagos penguins may join in a feeding free-for-all with boobies, gulls and shearwaters. In both of these scenarios, each kind of seabird uses a different feeding technique, such as surface feeding, plunge diving or pursuit diving, as is the case with penguins. In this way, the various seabirds lessen the competition among themselves.

Penguins are visual hunters. Most make their deepest dives at midday, presumably because this is the time when sunlight penetrates the water to the greatest depth and the birds are able to see farther. Even so, the depths reached by some kings and emperors are well beyond the reach of all but 1 or 2 percent of the sunlight. For all intents and purposes, then, these deep-diving birds are foraging in the dark.

Some penguins hunt at night. In one study of chinstraps on Signy Island, the birds were mainly nocturnal; some of the macaronis on South Georgia also forage after dark. In both cases, the birds fed on krill that migrated toward the surface at night. The eyes of penguins are not specifically adapted for nocturnal vision, so how is it that these birds are able to hunt at night and in the darkness of deep water? The answer lies in something known as bioluminescence.

Many krill, squid and some of the fish preyed upon by penguins have luminous spots scattered over their bodies. This biologically produced light results from the oxidation of a substance called luciferin, named after that most famous of pyromaniacs. Depending on the species and its role in the life of the owner, the light produced may be emitted as a single or repeated flash or a sustained glow. Bioluminescence may help an animal lure prey, attract a mate or keep a shoal together, and these benefits must outweigh the risk it poses in alerting hungry penguins to the animal's presence.

Penguins are superbly adapted to capture prey underwater. To begin with, the birds are fast and maneuverable. Humboldts studied in captivity could make turns using their tails, feet and laterally compressed beaks while traveling a distance of just one-quarter their body length. When a penguin is swimming, its neck is S-shaped, drawn into the hollow between its shoulders to make the bird more streamlined. When it strikes, it extends its neck rapidly, giving it a lightning reach to grab fast-swimming prey.

All penguins can swallow prey underwater and do it routinely over and over again during a single dive. This is a great benefit to them, because small schools of fish and krill can disperse quickly and valuable time would be lost if the penguin had to surface every time to swallow its catch. As well, the bird might have trouble finding the prey when it dove again. Even in dense schools of prey, a penguin does not plow through them with its mouth agape like a baleen whale filtering the water for edibles. Instead, it catches each item singly, no matter how small it is. Macaronis may catch 40 to 50 amphipods in this way in a single dive, chinstraps as many as 112 krill, and kings up to 29 lanternfish.

Krill and schooling fish have a strategy against penguins, but the birds often manage to get around it. Typically, schooling prey synchronize their swimming movements so that all the individuals face and move in the same direction. When they are polarized like this, it is more difficult for a predator to catch an individual, because the school reacts to an attack by withdrawing as a tight coordinated group and an individual is thus hard to single out. A hunting penguin's countertactic is to circle the school repeatedly to bunch the prey tighter and tighter until they become depolarized and the individuals start to act independently. In the resulting confusion, the prey is more vulnerable, and a penguin then dives beneath the school and swims through it from below, nabbing victims one after the other.

A penguin's eyes are best suited to sight above the line of its beak, so prey is best seen from below. As well, the dark plumage of a penguin's back seen from above against the depths of the ocean hides the bird's approach until it is too late for prey to react. The black-and-white striped pattern on the flanks of the four species of banded penguins may be a further help. The bold pattern may startle schools of fish when they are circled by the birds and make them depolarize that much faster. It's interesting to note that humpback whales (*Megaptera novaeangliae*) tighten swarms of krill by exhaling curtains of bubbles around them, after which they attack from below just as penguins do. Killer whales (*Orcinus orca*)

As illustrated by this little penguin, the eyes of all penguins sight above the bird's beak. This is helpful, since penguins commonly attack prey from below.

As in this rockhopper, the tongue and palate of every penguin are covered with stiff spines that keep food moving in one direction — inside.

off the coast of Norway use the same strategy against schools of Atlantic salmon.

The mouth of every penguin is a one-way trap. The tongue, the palate and even the upper throat are covered with stiff keratinized spines that improve the bird's grip on wiggly, slippery prey, and the spines point backward to keep food moving in one direction – inside. Swallowing prey underwater is virtually impossible to do without also swallowing a fair amount of salty seawater. Since the kidneys of a penguin are no better at excreting this salt load than are our own, the penguin, in common with all other seabirds, has two specialized salt glands to help it get rid of the extra salt it accidentally ingests. Each gland is the size of an almond, and there is one above each eye, cradled in a depression on the outside of the bird's skull. These salt glands drain into the penguin's nose, and when a bird first returns from the sea, drops of salty water run off the tip of its beak.

Although the general diet of every penguin includes a mix of the big three – fish, squid and crustaceans – its menu is more varied than it seems. The African penguin, for example, preys on 25 species of fish and 18 kinds of crustaceans, even though its primary food is shoaling pilchards and anchovies. The emperor eats three kinds of squid, five species of fish and four types of crustaceans. In the waters around Australia, the little penguin catches 28 different kinds of fish, one type of squid and one crustacean.

It's probably true that penguins will take whichever prey is available and easy to catch, and this may vary dramatically with location and season and from year to year. For example, gentoos studied on Marion Island ate mainly fish, while those on South Georgia ate krill. In another study showing seasonal variation, Australian little penguins devoured anchovies from January to June, pilchards from July to November and yet another species of fish in December. Probably the safest generalization to make about the diet of penguins is that they are generalists.

Not everything that scientists find in the stomachs of penguins is nutritious. Many species of penguins pick up pebbles from the beach or the ocean floor or scavenge gravel from the underside of floating glacial ice. In his 1842 journal, British explorer James Clark Ross wrote about this habit among emperors: "Their crops were frequently filled with pebbles. In one of these individuals, I found upwards of a pound [450 g] of small fragments of rocks, comprising basalt, greenstone, porphyry granite, vesicular lava, quartz, scoriae and pumice."

When emperor penguins travel
between the sea and their breeding colony they may have many
miles of ice to traverse.

One purpose of the rocks may be to help pulverize food in the bird's stomach. Nineteenth-century sealers and whalers believed that these rocks were ingested as ballast. More than 150 years after Ross's description, we are no closer to an answer, but the behavior has become an important part of antarctic history. Two years before Ross's voyage, an American expedition captured an emperor penguin, and the dissection of the bird forecast the discovery of the antarctic continent itself. The penguin was caught inside the Antarctic Circle at 66 degrees 52 minutes south latitude, and the basaltic pebbles the sailors found in the bird's stomach were interpreted as an indication of unknown antarctic lands. They were right.

Feeding competition among penguin species might seem to be a common occurrence. For instance, in the Falkland Islands, magellanics, gentoos and kings nest within 600 yards (550 m) of each other and leave on feeding trips from the same stretch of sandy beach. On the Antarctic Peninsula, where bare ground is scarce, all three brush-tailed penguins may nest in a variety of areas of the same colony and feed in the same offshore waters. Even so, competition among penguins is lessened in a number of ways.

Chunks of ice littering a shoreline may conceal a leopard seal ready to grab a penguin as it hops ashore.

When two crested penguin species nest on the same island, for example, it is always a small species and a large one that share the space, and the larger bird invariably starts its nesting cycle earlier. On Macquarie Island, macaronis arrive a month before the smaller rockhoppers, and on the Antipodes Islands, the larger erect-crested penguins lay three to four weeks before the resident rockhoppers. By staggering their breeding cycles, these different crested penguins use the food resources in succession rather than both trying to fledge chicks and fatten for their annual molt at exactly the same time.

Even when a number of penguin species simultaneously use the same area of ocean, they can reduce competition by searching for alternative prey or varying sizes of the same prey, by hunting at different times of the day and night and by diving to different water depths. Many researchers think that competition is most intense between the three brush-tailed penguins, which nest together in the islands of the Scotia Arc (South Georgia, South Orkney, South Sandwich). Krill make up more than 86 percent of their diets, and to decrease the overlap, penguins feed at a range of distances from their colonies. Gentoos feed closest to shore, no farther than 15 miles (24 km); chinstraps average 20½ miles (33 km); and Adélies forage the farthest, an average 31 miles (50 km). In some cases, the overlap may be even greater, and penguin species survive together simply because there is such an abundance of food that competition is not a factor.

The cue for a penguin to return to its colony may be the length of time that has elapsed rather than the fullness of its stomach. When prey is scarce, adults return to their chicks with less food in their stomachs. As a result, if a pair has two chicks, the smaller one may starve to death and the growth of the survivor may be slowed. In magellanic penguins on the coast of Argentina, for example, the chicks may fledge as soon as 60 days after hatching or as late as 120 days, depending entirely upon food availability. On the other hand, when food is plentiful, a foraging adult may stuff itself for the trip home. One Adélie captured in the Ross Sea had a belly-bulging 42,000 krill in its stomach. A penguin's stomach capacity is likely around 20 percent of its body weight, although they usually ingest half that amount.

Once penguins decide to return home, they waste very little time getting there. Occasionally, they start the return journey by making some searching dives, but they soon shift to travel dives on a course that is quite direct. As they near shore, they may shift once

again to porpoising as a strategy against predators. Often at this stage of the trip, the birds are tired and, laden with food for their chicks, may be less adroit at evading predators. This is when penguins are an easier target and at greatest risk.

Adélies often time their departure to coincide with the arrival of other groups returning safely from the sea.

Lions and Leopards

On December 4, 1995, I began my day at Volunteer Point in the Falkland Islands with these observations:

"As I arrived at the beach, a subadult male sea lion was in the water near shore shaking the carcass of a dead king penguin. Most of the time, the animal was submerged, and I could just make out the dark form of its body beneath the surface of the green water. A better indication of the sea lion's location was the throng of 12 to 14 giant petrels squabbling over bits and pieces of the dead

penguin that floated on the water. After eating only half of the penguin, the sea lion left the carcass, and the petrels swarmed over it immediately.

"While I was writing my notes, the same sea lion came ashore again and killed another king penguin. The predator ran out of the surf and up the beach for 250 to 300 feet [80–100 m], catching the fleeing penguin as it labored to climb a sandy embankment. By the time I noticed the animal, it was returning to the water with the king penguin dangling by its right shoulder and flipper from the animal's mouth. The tired sea lion humped back to the water in stages, moving five to six yards [5 m] at a time, then collapsing in a heap on its belly, presumably exhausted by the effort of the chase. Each rest spot was marked by a patch of blood in the wet sand. After four or five stops, the sea lion reached the upper wave line. The king penguin was still flapping wildly with its left flipper when the sea lion submerged beneath the foam, and I never saw the bird move again. The sea lion's head surfaced a few times, and each time, it gave the carcass a few violent shakes. At one point, it tossed the dead penguin into the air. The sea lion eventually abandoned the carcass without eating any of it and left it to the petrels. The whole event took less than 30 minutes."

I learned later that the same South American sea lion (*Otaria byronia*) had attacked two magellanic penguins earlier that morning, killing and eating one of the birds and seriously wounding the second one. Covered in blood, the surviving bird had escaped, run up the beach and disappeared into a burrow, where it probably died of its injuries. There have been many reports of such predation, and it seems that the South American sea lion hunts and kills every species of penguin which lives along the same shores as it does. But this species of sea lion is not the only penguin hunter. In the waters south of New Zealand, the fur seal (*Arctocephalus forsteri*) and Hooker sea lion (*Phocarctos hookeri*) prey on yellow-eyed penguins and on the different crested species. In Peru, South American fur seals (*Arctocephalus australis*) hunt Humboldt penguins, and on South Georgia, gangs of antarctic fur seals (*Arctocephalus gazella*) chase and kill kings, gentoos and macaronis.

Killer whales also prey on penguins as they leave and return to the beaches near their nesting colonies. On the Sea Lion Islands in the Falklands, I have watched pods of orcas swim within 50 feet (15 m) of the shore near the beach where a colony of gentoos regularly lands. I never witnessed the whales catch a penguin, but resident David Gray told me he had seen it often. In Îles Crozet,

This critically injured king penguin on South Georgia was probably attacked by a leopard seal. The seals routinely patrol the nesting beaches and prey on birds as they move in and out of the sea.

left: A large South American sea lion bull gapes menacingly at another bull in an adjacent territory. Sea lions evolved from a carnivore and are capable predators.

Although more than 60 percent of the diet of the leopard seal consists of krill and fish, it is its rapacious attacks on penguins that capture our attention.

killer whales gather offshore from the huge king penguin rookeries. In the award-winning film *Wolves of the Sea,* there is a remarkable sequence in which a killer whale catches a king penguin and plays with it, tossing the live bird into the air, then leaping clear of the water and batting the penguin through the air with a blow from its tail.

The mammalian penguin killer that outshadows all others is the 10-foot (3 m), 900-pound (400 kg) leopard seal of the Antarctic. Its scientific name, *Hydrurga leptonyx,* is Greek for slender, dark water worker, and work the water it does. At the huge Adélie colony at Cape Crozier, Antarctica, four leopard seals killed 15,000 penguins in a 15-week period, 5 percent of the breeding population. In another year in the same colony, half a dozen leopard seals killed 4,800 adults and 1,200 chicks. Individual killing rates can be quite high. In Prydz Bay, Antarctica, one proficient leopard seal huntress killed five Adélies in 134 minutes; on another occasion, she captured nine penguins in just 110 minutes.

Penguins are particularly vulnerable in rough seas when landings are made more difficult by the heavy surf. Predation rates, in fact, are four times higher in heavy-surf conditions than in light surf. Loose chunks of ice along the beach fringe can also create dangerous hazards for returning birds because the ice encumbers their swimming and makes the penguins easier prey for seals.

Leopard seals use five different hunting techniques. For one, they stalk the penguins under thin ice. In this case, an underwater seal follows a bird walking across newly formed ice, breaks through the ice, which is up to three inches (7.5 cm) thick, and nabs the unsuspecting bird. If the penguin spots the seal before it attacks, the bird may freeze with fear, remaining motionless for up to 80 minutes until it feels it is safe to continue.

Leopard seals also leap onto ice floes and try to grab any penguin that is standing near the edge. If there is no penguin close enough to catch, the seal may try to drive the birds off the safety of the ice, then pursue them in an underwater chase.

One of the two most common hunting methods is for a seal to lie quietly in the water near the shore, where it is hidden between pieces of ice as well as facing out to sea. Returning penguins literally swim into the seal's jaws. With emperors, a leopard seal may station itself on top of the ice beside a hole used by the birds to leave the water. The powerful seal, hidden from view, may grab an emperor in midair as it rockets from the water. The most common hunting strategy is for a leopard seal to patrol an ice edge where the penguins must leap up out of the water and onto the ice in order to reach the shore. Particularly when the water level is low, the birds may have to make many attempts before they succeed. The tired penguins are easy targets for lurking seals. Individual seals tend to specialize in one or two hunting methods and use those in preference to all others.

Researcher Dr. Gordon Court watched more than 100 kills of Adélies by these slender, dark water workers, observing that sometimes when a seal had already eaten, it would "toy with a debilitated penguin — mouthing it, pushing it around on the surface with its nose and frequently releasing it for short periods only to pull it back again and again from the safety of the floating ice."

When the seal wanted to kill the penguin quickly, it clenched the bird's head in its jaws and snapped the penguin's neck by jerking its body into the air. Sometimes, this would completely decapitate the penguin. Afterward, the seal would thrash the carcass on the surface of the water to separate the bird's body from its skin. On a feeding trip, a penguin may gain a couple of pounds of body fat, the greatest part of which is stored beneath its skin. Frequently, that is what the leopard seals selectively eat, leaving the discarded carcass to sink to the seafloor.

I studied northern bears for 10 years, and they practice a parallel behavior. When prey is abundant, a polar bear (*Ursus maritimus*) will eat only the blubber of the seals it catches, and the salmon-fishing brown bear (*Ursus arctos*) eats just the fat-rich brain, skin and eggs of its catches when the fishing is good. In all three predators, the rationale for the behavior is the same. A quantity of fat yields twice as much energy as an equal amount of either carbohydrate or protein, and a predator with a limited stomach capacity is best served by filling its stomach with energy-rich fat.

Moments before this photograph was taken, a leopard seal had lunged at these Adélie penguins as they stood on the ice close to the water. Immediately after the attack, the birds clambered beyond the range of the seal.

CHAPTER SIX

The Cycle Ends

The Graduating Class

For many penguin species, the breeding season represents a narrow window of opportunity during which a bird must find a mate, raise its chicks, fatten and molt—all before the seasonal pulse of food wanes. It is a race against time, and often, the deadline is winter. A chick that is late hatching, and is thus out of step, is doomed. No amount of parental care can swing the odds in its favor.

Most young penguins are finally abandoned by their parents when they are 2 to 4 months old. The obvious exception to this occurs with young kings, which don't fledge until they are 13 to 16 months old. Typically, the family bond breaks down fairly abruptly. Over the course of a week or two, first one parent stops its feeding visits, then the other. By this stage, the young penguins are no longer huddled in crèches; these have disbanded, and the birds either cluster in small parties at the edge of their colonies or loiter near the shoreline, watching the waves of adults come and go. Many of the young birds are molting the last of their natal down, and at this time, they are quite comical-looking. Tufts of down sprout from the tops of their heads like punk hairdos, and wispy strands still cling to their fresh new breast feathers like hair on the chest of a pubescent teenage boy.

The endearing appearance of the young penguins is matched by their flipper antics and their curious nature. At this age, the birds spend considerable time exercising their flippers, violently beating them back and forth through a range of movement so full that the

Adult penguins that have never bred, such as this gentoo, may go through the entire repertoire of courtship behaviors late in the season, when there is no possibility of a successful mating.

left: King penguin chicks take 13 to 16 months to fledge, three to four times longer than the young of most other penguin species. The chick shown here is finally shedding its downy coat.

The Cycle Ends 141

flippers almost touch each other on the upstroke. In the Falklands, a rainsquall once soaked me and a group of flipper-flexing king penguin chicks. I described the scene in my field notes: "When the rain hit, 100 or so brown fluffy chicks simultaneously began to run around beating their flippers excitedly, whistling loudly and snapping their beaks skyward to catch raindrops in their mouths. I would be tempted to caption a photograph of the scene with the words: 'I can fly, I can fly, I know I can fly if I can just beat these damn flippers of mine fast enough.'"

In keeping with their imminent independence, young penguins about to fledge are extremely curious, and nothing seems to stir this behavior more than a human and his gadgets. I've had young magellanic penguins peer inside my open camera bag with the intensity of the most absorbed photographer and lightly peck the contents. To young gentoos, a standing tripod seems to be irresistible. They immediately waddle over to investigate, and groups of 6 to 10 birds may cluster around the tripod as if paying homage to some long-legged avian deity. On occasion, young African penguins have wandered into author Cherry Kearton's tent, while a dozen more birds milled around outside.

My best interaction with young penguins has taken place when I sit perfectly still and let them come to me. An experience I recorded in my field notes about a gang of young gentoos was fairly typical: "Within a few minutes, six or seven nearly full-grown chicks rocked their way over to investigate. As they approached, they craned their necks in every conceivable direction, seemingly trying to decipher what kind of creature I was. After each bout of neck stretching, they would shuffle ahead a few steps and repeat the inspection all over again. If I moved suddenly, the penguins would squawk in alarm, run back a few feet, stop and look at me over their shoulders. In a few moments, their courage would return, and they would turn around and ease toward me once more. Eventually, one bold chick, the largest in the group, tugged gently at the sleeve of my jacket. Satisfied that I was neither edible nor dangerous, the daring chick turned away almost immediately and waddled off with its companions. Clearly, there were more interesting discoveries to be made in life."

The words of veteran penguin researcher Dr. Bernard Stonehouse sum up this effect perfectly: "I have had the impression that to penguins, man is just another penguin—different, less predictable, occasionally violent, but tolerable company when he sits still and minds his own business."

A young penguin must discover for itself the many hazards in its life, some of which can be quite unexpected. South Georgia, for instance, is home to more than 300,000 southern elephant seals. During the annual molting season, these gargantuan seals transform the natural bogs of the island into wallows. In the *Sierra Club Handbook of Seals and Sirenians,* seal experts Randall Reeves, Brent Stewart and Stephen Leatherwood write: "Some [elephant seals] die when they are unable to escape from the quicksand-like mud.... With its coating of mud, urine and feces, there are few things dead that smell as bad as a molting elephant seal alive."

Elephant seal wallows such as these can be especially hazardous to young penguins. The sides are steep and slippery, and any bird that happens to tumble in may be unable to escape. Twice, I have found the bodies of dead gentoos floating in the mire of these wallows, and I have almost fallen in myself. The only human I know who's slipped into the seal slop is my good friend Joe Van Os, who sank to his chest in the disgusting goo. After Joe had hauled himself out and trudged back to the ship, he looked and smelled so bad that the officers wouldn't let him come aboard until they had washed him down with one of the ship's fire hoses.

When a newly fledged magellanic penguin from the Falkland Islands fell over a cliff on its first trip to the ocean, its body was quickly claimed by a scavenging striated caracaras.

Two king penguin chicks, one still completely covered in down and the other just recently fledged, return from the sea after an exploratory outing.

Young penguins that have survived the risks of their early life move from land to sea over a relatively short period of time. According to one account, the newly fledged Adélie chicks from one colony in the Ross Sea were still all ashore on January 27. Within three days, 15 percent of them had left, and by February 2, half were gone. A week later, 97 percent of the penguins had left, and by February 15, none remained.

Early penguin observers concluded that adults lured their young to the water and taught them to swim before the family separated. Others stated that the chicks stayed onshore until starvation forced them into the ocean. Neither of these statements is correct. In fact, there are no preliminary swimming lessons with parents, and no adult bird feeds its young at sea. The young depart quite independent of their parents, although they may follow a group of adults, and many still have food residue in their stomachs, so it is unlikely that they have gone without eating for very long before they leave. In crowded beach areas, some chicks are simply shoved into the water accidentally when a group of adults leaves for the sea, or they are washed off the rocks by an unexpected wave.

Young penguins entering the water on their first trip to sea are unaware of the dangers posed by predators such as leopard seals. So when a seal lunges up at them from the water, they don't run back from the shore or the edge of the ice, and although they frequently leave land in the company of adults, their slow surface swimming makes them easy targets. In February and March, the sea is full of floundering chicks, and the hunting is good for the seals. Even so, because the chicks depart in a fairly synchronized fashion, their numbers swamp the predators, and as a result, fewer of them are killed.

After the barrage of flooded nests, freezing rains, blizzards, neighborhood brawls, extended fasts and predatory fangs, talons and beaks, how many penguin chicks actually live to graduate to the sea? As with so many aspects of a penguin's life, its breeding success varies with location and from year to year. Some seasons, a bumper crop of chicks swims out to sea, while other years are total failures. Consider little penguins in Australia. In good years, when food is plentiful, 39 percent of pairs raise two chicks, compared with only 13 percent in poor years. But even in bumper years, 38 percent of pairs do not raise any chicks at all, and that number rises to a dismal 54 percent in bad years.

In Chapter 4, I discuss the huge egg and chick losses — sometimes exceeding 90 percent — that can take place in antarctic colonies

This emperor penguin chick is now about three months old. It will be another two months before it finally sheds its downy coat and is on its own.

of Adélies and emperors because of foul weather and heavy ice conditions. But similarly devastating nest failures can occur in penguins that breed in much more clement latitudes as well. For example, among gentoos on South Georgia, the success rate for fledging chicks varies between 1.2 chicks per pair at the best of times and zero in the worst years. During one particularly bad breeding season, only one gentoo chick fledged in an entire colony of 3,000 pairs.

Even among penguins of the same species, breeding on the same island, the success rate can vary. Consider gentoos again, only this time a population from Macquarie Island. Gentoo colonies containing 1 to 50 nests fledged 0.8 chicks per pair, and that rate improved to 1.17 chicks per pair in colonies which contained 250 to 300 nests. The difference in success is likely due to a difference in nest vulnerability to predators, especially to skuas. Larger colonies have a smaller percentage of nests on the perimeter of the colony, which is the most dangerous location and the most difficult to defend.

How have penguins survived millions of years when they frequently have such pitiful breeding success? Like many seabirds, penguins have relatively long life spans. It's possible that an emperor could live for 50 years, although the oldest on record is a captive 34-year-old bird. The life span records for most other species are around 20 years, and the records for maximum breeding age are almost as high: 19 years for a yellow-eyed penguin, 17 for a little penguin and 20 for an Adélie. Penguins may not begin breeding until they are 5 or 6 years old, but given that late start, their breeding life is still longer than that of most birds. And because they have such long reproductive lives, it is not a tragedy when a single breeding season — or two or even three — fails. To maintain the population size, each penguin simply needs to replace itself and raise one chick to maturity during its lifetime.

Just when I thought the list of natural hardships and hazards that a penguin faces in raising its chicks could get no longer, I heard about one more in Africa. The story was related to me by Dr. David Cameron Duffy. In 1986, a small mainland colony of African penguins in Betty's Bay, South Africa, was on the increase. Among biologists, that fact was one of the few reasons for optimism in a penguin population which was declining in many other regions. One night, 50 birds — roughly half of the members of the colony — were killed by a leopard (*Panthera pardus*). All were left uneaten. Two nights later, the big cat returned and killed another 15 birds. The colony has still not recovered.

The Big Meltdown

From an energy standpoint, most birds have three big expenses in their lives: reproduction, migration and molting. For penguins, molting is by far the most costly of the three. At the end of the annual breeding season, every adult leaves the colony and goes to sea for an intense period of feeding and fattening. The length of time spent doing this varies among species and ranges from several weeks in little penguins and some of the crested penguins to several months in yellow-eyes, kings and emperors. The variability partly reflects differences in body size among the species, but it is also a function of the differences in food availability. For example, macaroni penguins from Marion Island take twice as long to fatten as those from the food-rich waters around South Georgia. For each species, the period at sea also varies from year to year. In years when food is scarce, magellanic penguins from coastal Argentina may not molt until May, two to three months later than normal.

It is very late in the nesting season, and although this magellanic chick looks strong and healthy, its growth is seriously out of synchrony with the other young penguins in the colony. It will probably not survive.

Young emperor penguin chicks frequently move around within the breeding colony. Sometimes they move more than a mile (1.6 km) in a day.

It is frequently assumed that most penguins fatten in the same areas of the ocean where they foraged while feeding their chicks. In fact, they may travel far greater distances. Macaronis from Marion Island, for instance, range between 36 miles (60 km) and 186 miles (300 km) when feeding their chicks. During the pre-molt feeding binge, two male penguins from the same islands traveled 885 miles (1,425 km) and 1,470 miles (2,360 km), respectively.

When they eventually return from the sea, the corpulent penguins are the fattest they will be at any time of the year. Some may have doubled their body weight and be so plump and padded that they can barely climb up the shoreline to reach a resting spot. Most yellow-eyed and crested penguins molt in the nest sites they used earlier in the season and are accompanied by their mate of that year. The partners may preen each other, engage in vocal and postural displays and even copulate — all of which strengthens the bond between them and reinforces their fidelity for the next breeding season. Little and banded penguins often molt in a secluded spot along the shoreline or hide in a burrow, not necessarily the one they occupied while breeding. Among the brush-tailed penguins, gentoos and most chinstraps molt at their colonies, though not at their nests, but Adélies stay out on the sea ice in the shelter of a pressure ridge or hop aboard an iceberg and take a slow float to nowhere. Emperors also stay on the sea ice to molt, while kings shuffle back to their colonies and cluster in molting clubs.

A penguin about to molt is relatively easy to recognize: Its feathers are faded, and its normally deep black plumage turns brownish. At Islas Los Choros, off the coast of Chile, all of the adult Humboldt penguins I saw along the shoreline were bleached and discolored in that way. With binoculars, I could see that their feather tips were worn and frayed. In molting Galápagos penguins and others, the birds' flippers, engorged with blood, swell to twice their normal size and bruise and bleed easily when bumped.

Molting penguins are surprisingly quiet and much less quarrelsome than they are during the breeding season. Their calm demeanor helps them to conserve energy, and if ever a penguin needs to be energetically frugal, it is during the molt. In most species, it takes the birds two to four weeks to replace their feathers, but in the large kings and emperors, it may require four to six weeks. Weight losses during the molting period are extreme, ranging from 35 to 50 percent of a penguin's pre-molt weight.

Consider the weight changes recorded in a study of Australian little penguins. At the start of the molt, on February 15, the birds weighed an average of 4 pounds (1.8 kg). A week later, they had dropped to 3½ pounds (1.5 kg), and by February 28, they had thinned down to just over 2½ pounds (1.2 kg). When the birds completed their three-week molt on March 7, they weighed only 2 pounds (1 kg), a 50 percent loss in weight. During their molt, little penguins — and probably many other species as well — lose twice as much weight per day as they do during the breeding season, when they are fasting. Why does molting require so much energy?

All penguins fast when they are molting, so they must draw on stored energy reserves to fuel their basic metabolism while they are ashore. In addition, they must replace every feather on their bodies, and that is where the added cost comes in. Feathers are mainly keratin, a type of protein, and the amino acids required to build the keratin are drawn from the bird's other body proteins. In an emperor penguin, that amounts to two pounds (1 kg) of feather proteins, and virtually all that protein is purloined from the penguin's

An exceedingly fat king penguin returns to its colony on South Georgia to undergo its annual molt.

The brownish feathers on these Humboldt penguins in coastal Chile have been bleached and damaged by the intense sun. The birds are about to molt.

right: It is late January in the Falkland Islands, and a rockhopper penguin chick finally molts its down. By this time of year, many of the young penguins have been abandoned by their parents and are reluctantly independent.

muscles. An emperor, in fact, loses half of its body protein during the annual molt—most of it from the powerful flipper muscles on its chest. At the end of the molt, the bony keel on the sternum of many penguins is clearly visible beneath the bird's new plumage.

The molting pattern of penguins is unique among birds. Some auks and waterfowl become flightless, but none lose all their feathers at once, and none are forced to stay out of the water. A molting penguin temporarily forfeits much of the insulation that its feathers provide. If it went into the water, it would lose excessive amounts of body heat and its temperature would drop. For example, when a molting Galápagos penguin was placed in water at 70°F (21°C)—a temperature typical of the area—its body temperature went from 107°F (42°C) to 97°F (36°C) in just 30 seconds. The chilled penguin immediately scrambled back onto the land.

There is another reason for a molting penguin to stay on shore—the effect of increased drag. While a penguin is shedding its

A king penguin may fast for over a month while it molts. During this time, it can lose half of its body weight, a practical reason for the bird to fatten up as much as possible beforehand.

old feathers, it loses its normal streamlined profile and the frayed plumage adds to the drag on its body when the bird is swimming. A slower penguin has a harder time catching prey and evading predators and, for both of these reasons, is better off sitting on shore. Sometimes, however, a penguin has no choice but to go back into the water. The drastic weight losses these birds commonly endure are those usually associated with terminal starvation in other birds. If the fat reserves of a molting penguin are inadequate to sustain it until its feathers are fully replaced, it must leave the land and take whatever risks are necessary in order to feed.

In a colony of penguins, not all the adults molt at the same time. Nonbreeders molt first, then the failed breeders and, finally, the successful breeders. The reasons for this are easy to understand. Breeding adults are preoccupied with feeding their chicks and must delay their molt until after their offspring fledge. The other adult groups have no such constraints and can molt earlier. Even though it is staggered, the timing of the molt for most of the adults still works to the benefit of the newly fledged chicks. Many adults are confined to shore molting when the greatest number of young penguins are first going to sea. This gives the chicks at least a few weeks when they do not have to compete with experienced adults for a declining food supply. By the time the adults return to the water, the chicks are more proficient at finding and catching food and, presumably, more resilient to competition.

Molting in the Galápagos penguin is different enough from the other species to merit a few extra words. The Galápagos penguin molts twice each year rather than once, as in all other species, which is seemingly a tremendous drain on its reserves. Scientists speculate that the added burden is probably necessary because the strength of the equatorial sun bleaches and damages the bird's feathers faster than in those species which live in temperate and polar latitudes.

The molt of the Galápagos penguin differs in another way: it *precedes* the breeding season rather than following it, as is the case in all other species. This can be explained by the extreme unpredictability of the Galápagos penguin's food supply. Periodic influxes of warm water, called an El Niño event, prevent the usual cold-water upwelling from occurring in the islands. As a result, ocean-food production drops dramatically. Breeding Galápagos penguins have no way of knowing when an El Niño will strike or how long one will last. If they were to breed first, when ocean conditions were good, but were then struck by an El Niño, they might

be unable to fatten enough to complete their molt. By molting first, the adults survive in the event of a sudden change in ocean conditions to breed another time, even though their chicks may perish.

The molting period for most penguin species concludes the annual phase of a penguin's life, the time during which it is tied to the land and about which we know the most. But the penguin is a seabird, and for more than half of the species, the time has come to migrate to sea and disappear into the black hole of the unknown. As technology continues to advance, scientists undoubtedly will slowly unlock the mysteries of the penguin's life at sea, adding further to the scientific and aesthetic appeal of this unique family of birds.

I know that the science and beauty of penguins will be part of my life forever. As antarctic adventurer Apsley Cherry-Garrard wrote: "You must agree that a bird like this is an interesting beast."

During the annual molt, a king penguin not only replaces all the feathers on its body but, a month or so later, also replaces the salmon-colored plate on its lower beak.

A rockhopper cautiously approaches the edge of its colony in the Falkland Islands

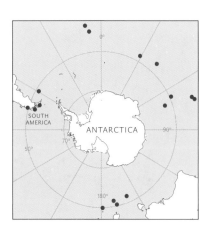

Penguins of the World

Rockhopper Penguin

(*Eudyptes chrysocome*)

Distribution: The rockhopper is the smallest of the crested penguins, yet it is tolerant to the greatest range of temperatures and, as a result, has the widest distribution of any of the six crested penguins. The rockhopper breeds between 37 and 53 degrees south latitude throughout the circumpolar sub-Antarctic. Three subspecies are recognized: *E.c. chrysocome*, which breeds on islands clustered around Cape Horn and on the Falkland Islands; *E.c. filholi* on Îles Crozet, Îles Kerguélen and Marion, Heard, Macquarie, Campbell, Auckland and Antipodes islands; and the northern rockhopper, *E.c. moseleyi*, found on Île Saint-Paul and Tristan da Cunha, Gough and Amsterdam islands. The rockhopper is absent from its breeding islands from April to September, but its winter range is poorly known.

Breeding Population: 2 million pairs.

Status: Stable after widespread declines in recent years.

Fiordland Penguin

(*Eudyptes pachyrhynchus*)

Distribution: The fiordland penguin nests only along the southwestern coast of the South Island of New Zealand and on nearby Stewart Island. The habitat consists of lush temperate rainforests complete with giant tree ferns. The bird is absent from its colony between March and June while it forages in New Zealand's offshore waters.

Breeding Population: 2,500-3,000, but may be fewer than 1,000.

Status: Dramatic declines since the turn of the century. Currently threatened, but the bird's exact status is unknown because the dense vegetation of its habitat makes estimates extremely difficult.

Photograph © Frank Todd

Snares Penguin

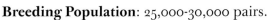
(*Eudyptes robustus*)

Distribution: The Snares penguin breeds only on The Snares, a group of islands roughly 124 miles (200 km) south of New Zealand and barely 620 acres (250 ha) in extent. Set amid forests of giant tree daisies, the nesting colonies are empty from May to August while the birds are at sea.

Breeding Population: 25,000-30,000 pairs.
Status: Stable or increasing.

Erect-crested Penguin

(*Eudyptes sclateri*)

Distribution: Two clusters of islands southeast of New Zealand – the Antipodes and the Bounty islands – are the main breeding areas of the erect-crested penguin, although some birds also nest on the nearby Auckland Islands. In common with most of the other eudyptid penguins, the erect-crested vacates its colonies in the winter and is absent from May to September.

Breeding Population: 150,000-175,000 pairs.
Status: Declining.

Macaroni Penguin

(*Eudyptes chrysolophus*)

Distribution: The macaroni penguin is the most abundant penguin in the world. It nests in the South Atlantic and Indian oceans and breeds farther south than any other crested penguin, even reaching the Antarctic Peninsula. The main breeding populations are on South Georgia, Îles Crozet, Îles Kerguélen and Heard and Macquarie islands, each of which has from one to five million breeding pairs. The bird leaves the colony in April or May and usually does not return until October.

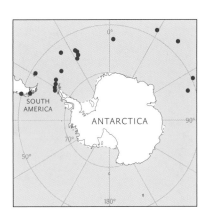

Breeding Population: 10 million pairs.
Status: Declining in parts of its range, especially around South Georgia.

Royal Penguin

(*Eudyptes schlegeli*)

Distribution: The royal penguin breeds only on Macquarie Island, an Australian protectorate approximately 900 miles (1,450 km) southeast of Hobart, Tasmania, and roughly halfway between there and the coast of Antarctica. The royal is absent from Macquarie Island for four months during the height of the austral winter.

Breeding Population: 850,000 pairs in 57 colonies.

Status: Stable.

Magellanic Penguin

(*Spheniscus magellanicus*)

Distribution: The main breeding range of the magellanic penguin skirts the southern tip of South America, from 42 degrees south latitude on the Atlantic Coast of Argentina, around Cape Horn, then north along the coast of Chile, reaching 29 degrees south. A small breeding population of magellanic penguins is also found on the Falkland Islands. In winter, the Pacific Coast birds migrate as far north as Peru and those along the Atlantic Coast move to the offshore waters of Brazil.

Breeding Population: 1.3 million pairs.

Status: Stable.

Humboldt Penguin

(*Spheniscus humboldti*)

Distribution: The Humboldt penguin, named after the cold, rich current flowing north along the western coast of South America, breeds along the coastline and on the offshore islands of Chile and Peru, between 33 and 5 degrees south latitude. Adults remain near their colonies year-round. The breeding range of Humboldts and magellanics overlaps for about 280 miles (450 km) along the central coast of Chile.

Breeding Population: Fewer than 5,000 pairs.

Status: Vulnerable to El Niño events and overfishing in the Humboldt Current.

Galápagos Penguin

(*Spheniscus mendiculus*)

Distribution: The Galápagos penguin, the smallest and most tropical of the banded penguins, is endemic to the Galápagos Islands. The birds are year-round residents of the archipelago and breed mainly on Fernandina and the western and northern coasts of Isabela, where the rich upwelling of the cold Cromwell Current supports the population.

Breeding Population: 1,200-1,500 pairs.

Status: Endangered and highly vulnerable to recurrent El Niño events.

African or Jackass Penguin

(*Spheniscus demersus*)

Distribution: The jackass penguin is the only penguin found in Africa, and it breeds mainly on inshore islands along the southern coast of South Africa as far north as the southwestern coast of Namibia. It is a year-round resident.

Breeding Population: 56,000 pairs, a decline from 500,000 pairs at the turn of the century.

Status: Vulnerable.

Adélie Penguin

(*Pygoscelis adeliae*)

Distribution: The Adélie is the little black-and-white penguin of Antarctica that most of us think of when we think of penguins. It breeds along the peninsula and around most of the perimeter of the continent. Because it breeds farther south than any other penguin species (77 degrees south latitude), it spends the least amount of time at its nesting colony, just four to five months each year. The rest of the time, it is at sea, along the northern edge of the pack ice.

Breeding Population: 2.47 million pairs.

Status: Stable, with increases in some populations—possibly secondary to a warming trend in the Southern Ocean.

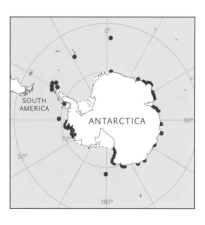

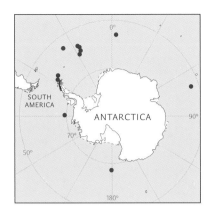

Chinstrap Penguin

(*Pygoscelis antarctica*)

Distribution: The chinstrap penguin is the second most abundant penguin on Earth. Ninety-five percent of the birds breed on the islands of the Scotia Arc, especially on the South Sandwich Islands, where there are an estimated five million pairs. The chinstrap is absent from its colony from May to September and presumably disperses to the northern edge of the antarctic pack ice.

Breeding Population: 7.49 million pairs.

Status: Stable or slightly increasing, possibly the result of a warming trend in the Southern Ocean.

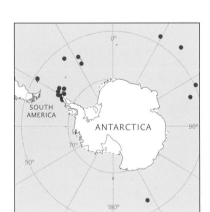

Gentoo Penguin

(*Pygoscelis papua*)

Distribution: The gentoo penguin, the largest of the brush-tailed group, breeds on most of the subantarctic islands, from the Falklands east to Macquarie, but is absent from all the island groups south of New Zealand. This is the northern gentoo (*P.p. papua*). The other subspecies, the southern gentoo (*P.p. ellsworthii*), nests in the islands of the Scotia Arc and on the Antarctic Peninsula as far south as Petermann Island, at 65 degrees 10 minutes south latitude, just short of the Antarctic Circle. At most of the breeding colonies, some birds are present throughout the year.

Breeding Population: 314,000 pairs.

Status: Stable.

Emperor Penguin

(*Aptenodytes forsteri*)

Distribution: The emperor is the only penguin that may never touch land in its lifetime. The most cold-adapted of the 17 species, it breeds along the antarctic coast in 42 known colonies, all but five of which are within the Antarctic Circle and none north of 64 degrees.

Breeding Population: 218,000 pairs.

Status: Stable.

King Penguin

(*Aptenodytes patagonicus*)

Distribution: The king penguin is a bird of the sub-Antarctic, breeding from Cape Horn east to Macquarie Island. There are no colonies south of 60 degrees. Two subspecies are recognized: *A.p. patagonicus*, which breeds on South Georgia, the Falklands and Cape Horn, and *A.p. halli*, which breeds on Îles Crozet, Îles Kerguélen and Prince Edward and Macquarie islands, each of which has between 70,000 and 500,000 nesting pairs.

Breeding Population: 1.5 million pairs.

Status: Stable with recent increases on Îles Crozet, Îles Kerguélen and Heard Island.

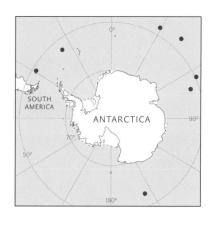

Yellow-eyed Penguin

(*Megadyptes antipodes*)

Distribution: The yellow-eyed penguin nests on Stewart, Auckland and Campbell islands, off the southeastern coast of the South Island of New Zealand. This large penguin is the most endangered of all the species, with the smallest estimated breeding population. The bird is present at its colony throughout the year.

Breeding Population: 2,000 pairs.

Status: Endangered.

Little or Fairy Penguin

(*Eudyptula minor*)

Distribution: The little penguin breeds around the entire perimeter of New Zealand, along the coast of Tasmania and all along the southern coast of the Australian mainland. The little penguin rarely strays far from its breeding colony and can be found nearby throughout the year. Six subspecies are recognized, but these are being reevaluated.

Breeding Population: 250,000 pairs.

Status: Stable but may be declining.

King penguins now number over one million pairs, and the population has recently increased on several island groups.

The Southern Hemisphere

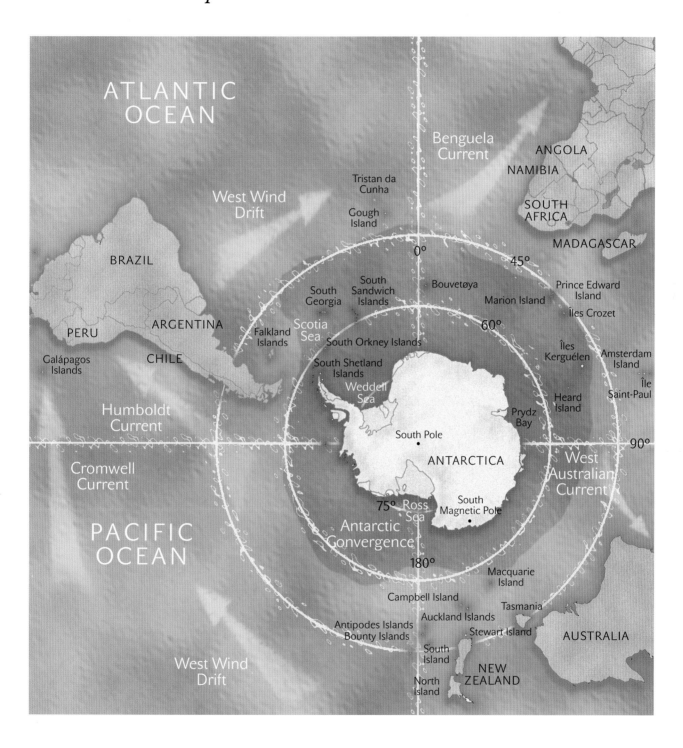

ATLANTIC
OCEAN

Benguela
Current

ANGOLA

NAMIBIA

SOUTH
AFRICA

MADAGASCAR

West Wind
Drift

Tristan da
Cunha

Gough
Island

0°

45°

BRAZIL

South
Georgia

South
Sandwich
Islands

Bouvetøya

Marion Island

Prince Edward
Island

Îles Crozet

PERU

ARGENTINA

CHILE

Scotia
Sea

Falkland
Islands

South Orkney Islands

60°

Îles
Kerguélen

Amsterdam
Island

Galápagos
Islands

South Shetland
Islands

Weddell
Sea

Île
Saint-Paul

Heard
Island

Humboldt
Current

Prydz
Bay

South Pole

ANTARCTICA

90°

West
Australian
Current

Cromwell
Current

South
Magnetic Pole

75° Ross
Sea

PACIFIC
OCEAN

Antarctic
Convergence

180°

Macquarie
Island

Campbell Island

Tasmania

Auckland Islands

Antipodes Islands
Bounty Islands

Stewart Island

AUSTRALIA

South
Island

NEW
ZEALAND

West Wind
Drift

North
Island

Penguins and People

Humans have never been kind to penguins. From the moment European sailors spotted them in the late 15th century, penguins and their eggs were regularly on the menu. Uncounted thousands were bludgeoned, salted and barreled. But these early seafarers were amateurs in the decimation business. Not until the early 1800s did the professionals arrive and show them how it could be done.

It began with a chance discovery by Captain James Cook in 1775. The famous explorer was the first to report the multitudes of antarctic fur seals that crammed the beaches of South Georgia. For the next century, wooden ships reeking of blood and death rolled and pitched across every corner of the Southern Ocean. Millions of fur seals were skinned for their luxuriant pelts, and countless elephant seals were butchered and boiled for their precious lard.

At first, on the treeless islands where the sealers slaughtered their quarry, penguins were killed as cordwood to fuel the boiling pots. But when the numbers of blubbery seals began to dwindle, the abundant birds became a logical substitute. In just two years, 1864 to 1866, 63,000 gallons (238,500 l) of penguin oil were shipped from the port of Stanley, in the Falkland Islands. Since it takes the boiled bodies of at least eight rockhoppers to yield a gallon of oil (two for a liter), that means roughly 500,000 penguins were killed and cooked. In the next 14 years, as many as 1.5 million rockhoppers were tossed into digesters and rendered into lamp oil.

The glint of gold has often spurred humankind to heights of barbarity. Soon after the first sealers arrived on Macquarie Island in the 1820s, hundreds of thousands of royal and king penguins were sentenced to a hideous death. The men herded droves of the terrified and defenseless birds up makeshift wooden ramps. Many of the penguins were year-old birds, called "fats," that had returned to the security of the island to molt. At the end of the gangplank, the hapless birds tumbled into caldrons of boiling oil. Imagine the noise, the stench and the spectacle. But it wasn't sudden enlightenment that halted the slaughter; it was just the decline of profit as penguin numbers slumped below commercially viable levels.

It might have been easy to dismiss the actions of these early sealers as coarse and vile and to take sanctuary on higher moral ground, but regrettably, subsequent generations have fallen from that moral perch. Twentieth-century explorers and scientists have proved themselves to be as guilty of such exploitation as any.

In 1902, geologist Dr. Otto Nordenskjöld wintered with a party on the eastern coast of the Antarctic Peninsula. Although he decried the killing of penguins, he and the men with him cooked and ate hundreds of the birds. A typical menu for a week included: cold penguin and sardines; salted penguin; macaroni and salted penguin; breast of penguin and dried vegetables; salted penguin and beans; and pastry with leftover penguin.

In 1948, the year I was born, Dr. William Sladen was in Antarctica conducting his pioneering research on Adélie penguins. Besides gaining insight into the lives of these fascinating seabirds, the resourceful scientist also discovered that they made excellent dog

Curious king penguins surround Aubrey Lang, the author's wife, on a beach on South Georgia Island.

food. Sladen killed over 2,000 Adélie and chinstrap penguins to feed his team of sled dogs. As recently as the early 1980s, scientists at Argentina's Esperanza Base in Antarctica also fed penguins to their dogs. Sled dogs were brought to many scientific stations on the continent, often for recreational use as much as anything. The high-strung canids frequently escaped from their chains and often ravaged nearby penguin colonies in killing sprees that claimed dozens of penguin lives. Thankfully, the last sled dogs were finally shipped home from the continent in the early 1990s.

Why should anyone worry about the fate of a few thousand penguins when presumed national interest is at stake? Most nations which have made an investment in Antarctica will say that you shouldn't. Many of the stations on the continent are perched along shorelines that are free of ice and snow in summer. These also happen to be the few locations where penguins can nest. At Pointe Géologie, the French built an airstrip right through the center of an Adélie colony. At Cape Hallett, the United States and New Zealand were undoubtedly equally remorseful when they built their own station and bulldozed yet another Adélie colony, this time evicting 8,000 penguins, including 3,300 molting chicks.

Human awareness seems to be slow in coming to penguinland—possibly it's the cold that dulls our sensoria. In 1990, an aircraft servicing the Australian research base on Macquarie Island carelessly flew low over a large colony of breeding king penguins, causing them to stampede. The result: 1,000 adults and 6,000 terrified chicks suffocated after piling up 10-deep against a barrier of rock and tussock grass.

On the other hand, modern-day tourists may be *loving* penguins to death. Antarctic tourism began in earnest in 1970 with the first voyages of the "little red ship," the *M.S. Lindblad Explorer*, a 90-passenger adventure cruise ship. Since then, the trickle of passengers has become a steady stream. In the 2005–2006 tourist season, 26,245 passengers sailed on 37 different ships to the shores of the frozen continent, and all of them wanted to see penguins.

For many years, scientists argued about the impact that visiting tourists had on a penguin colony. In 1996, Melissa Giese published the results of her interesting study on the breeding success of Adélie penguins and the impact of tourist visits as well as scientists checking the birds' nests. Giese concluded that both tourists *and* scientists can have a great influence on the number of chicks a pair of Adélies can raise. The disturbance was greatest in small colonies, where chick losses were 72 percent or higher for nests visited by either tourists or scientists. In large colonies, the impact was far less, and chick mortality increased by just 2 to 11 percent in visited nests. In both large and small colonies, the chicks died either because visitors caused adults to desert the nests or because they disturbed the birds long enough for a skua to prey on the defenseless young.

As I have chronicled, in the history of humans and penguins, we have boiled and foiled them and never once done anything to improve their lot, except possibly when we were repairing damage we had caused in the first place. Sadly, oiling is yet another way humans have affected the lives of penguins. In 1994, more than 2,600 tons of fuel oil spilled off the coast of South Africa, affecting 40,000 African penguins. Every year along the 1,860-mile (3,000 km) coastline of Argentina, more than 20,000 adult and 22,000 juvenile magellanics die from oil pollution leaked from ships and pipelines.

Global warming will have an impact on the entire planet, but the temperature increases will be greatest in the polar regions. Across Antarctica, air temperatures have already increased by 0.9 to 1.8°F (0.5–1°C), and climate models project they may eventually increase by 9°F (5°C) or more on the Antarctic Peninsula—the most clement portion of the continent. Ocean temperatures have warmed as well. The climate warming in the peninsula has led to the disintegration of regional ice shelves, exposing more land, as well as a reduction in winter sea ice in the nearby Bellingshausen and Amundsen seas. As far as scientists know, no new penguin colony has been founded as a result of the increase in bare land, but the number of Adèlie penguins on the peninsula has declined in the past decade. On the other hand, the number of chinstraps penguins have increased.

Is there any good news? Well, there is some. In 1991, the signatory nations to the Antarctic Environmental Protocol decreed that the continent shall be "a natural reserve devoted to peace and science." As part of this formal declaration of conservation, many scientific bases have begun to monitor and lessen their impact on local wildlife. The greatest hope for penguins, however, rests in humanity's increasing realization that policies and actions designed to protect wildlife are the surest way to protect and preserve our own future.

Magellanic penguins wait in the shallows of a tidepool watching a juvenile southern sea lion loafing on the beach.

Further Reading

Books and technical journals are an addiction with me, and I'm disappointed if I'm unable to read for at least three or four hours every day. The natural sciences — in particular, animal behavior — are the subjects that interest me most. While preparing for this book, I read extensively on the ecology and biology of penguins and other seabirds, as well as the fascinating natural history of Antarctica and the Southern Ocean. All the books I have listed here should be available at most community libraries through interlibrary loan. I will always remember the words of a wise English teacher I had when I was in high school: "There's never any excuse to know less than you want to know about anything. Use the library."

Ainley, David G. *The Adélie Penguin — Bellweather of Climate Change.* New York: Columbia University Press, 2002.

Ainley, David G., Robert E. LeResche and William J.L. Sladen. *Breeding Biology of the Adélie Penguin.* Berkeley: University of California, 1983.

Bonner, W.N., and D.W.H. Walton (editors). *Key Environments — Antarctica.* New York: Pergamon Press, 1985.

Campbell, David G. *The Crystal Desert — Summers in Antarctica.* Boston: Houghton Mifflin Company, 1992.

Capricorn Press (editors). *Antarctica — The Extraordinary History of Man's Conquest of the Frozen Continent,* 2nd edition. Sydney: Reader's Digest, 1990.

Cherry-Garrard, Apsley. *The Worst Journey in the World.* London: Penguin Books, 1922.

Cooper, J. (editor). Proceedings of the Third International Penguin Conference. *Marine Ornithology,* Vol. 27. Rhodes Gift 7707, South Africa: African Seabird Group, 1999.

Croxall, J.P. (editor). *Seabirds: Feeding Ecology and Role in Marine Ecosystems.* New York: Cambridge, 1987.

Dann, Peter, Ian Norman and Pauline Reilly (editors). *The Penguins: Biology and Management.* Surrey Beatty & Sons, 1995.

Davis, Lloyd S., and John T. Darby (editors). *Penguin Biology.* New York: Academic Press Inc., 1990.

Davis, Lloyd S. and Martin Renner. *Penguins.* London: T & AD Poyser, 2003.

Gill, Frank B. *Ornithology*, 2nd edition. New York: W.H. Freeman and Company, 1995.

Kearton, Cherry. *The Island of Penguins.* New York: Robert M. McBride & Co., 1931.

Knox, George A. *The Biology of the Southern Ocean.* Cambridge: Cambridge University Press, 1994.

Kooyman, Gerald L. *Diverse Divers, Physiology and Behavior.* London: Springer-Verlag, 1989.

Laws, R.M. (editor). *Antarctic Ecology, Volumes 1 & 2.* New York: Academic Press, 1984.

Moss, Sanford. *Natural History of the Antarctic Peninsula.* New York: Columbia University Press, 1988.

Müller-Schwarze, Dietland. *The Behavior of Penguins Adapted to Ice and Tropics.* Albany: State University of New York Press, 1984.

Murphy, Robert Cushman. *Oceanic Birds of South America, Volumes 1 & 2.* New York: American Museum of Natural History, 1936.

Nelson, Bryan. Seabirds, *Their Biology and Ecology.* New York: A & W Publishers, 1979.

Sladen, William J.L. *The Pygoscelid Penguins I. Methods of Study II. The Adélie Penguin.* Falkland Islands Dependencies Survey Scientific Report No. 17, 1958.

Stonehouse, Bernard (editor). *The Biology of Penguins*. London: University Park Press, 1975.

Stonehouse, Bernard. *The Emperor Penguin (Aptenodytes forsteri) I. Breeding Behaviour and Development*. Falkland Islands Dependencies Survey Scientific Report No.6, 1953.

———. *The King Penguin (Aptenodytes patagonica) of South Georgia I. Breeding Behaviour and Development*. Falkland Islands Dependencies Survey Scientific Report No.23, 1960.

———. *North Pole, South Pole*. Toronto: McGraw-Hill Ryerson, 1990.

———. *Polar Ecology*. New York: Chapman and Hall, 1989.

Williams, Tony D. *The Penguins*. New York: Oxford University Press, 1995.

Young, Euan. *Skua and Penguin: Predator and Prey*. Cambridge: Cambridge University Press, 1994.

King penguins cross the swift waters of a glacial meltwater stream. The birds are often knocked over by the strength of the current and complete the crossing by swimming.

Index

Page numbers in italics refer to illustrations
Page numbers followed by 't' refer to tables.